Robert Rogers' Rules for the Ranging Service

An Analysis

Matt Wulff

HERITAGE BOOKS
2007

HERITAGE BOOKS

AN IMPRINT OF HERITAGE BOOKS, INC.

Books, CDs, and more—Worldwide

For our listing of thousands of titles see our website
at
www.HeritageBooks.com

Published 2007 by
HERITAGE BOOKS, INC.
Publishing Division
65 East Main Street
Westminster, Maryland 21157-5026

Copyright © 2006 Matt Wulff

All rights reserved. No part of this book may be reproduced or
transmitted in any form or by any means, electronic or mechanical,
including photocopying, recording or by any information storage
and retrieval system without written permission from the author,
except for the inclusion of brief quotations in a review.

International Standard Book Number: 978-0-7884-3376-4

Contents

Maps, Photographs and Diagrams

All photographs were taken by Matt Wulff,
Beth Wulff, Dan Schroth, Paul Meier, and Thomas Pray.
Dan, Paul and Thomas are members of the New York Company of
Jaeger's Battalion.

All diagrams were hand drawn by Matt Wulff.

Diagrams:

Acknowledgments

This book was born out of a project I worked on towards the development of a tactical manual for the reenactment group that I belong to, Jaeger's Battalion of Rogers Rangers, headquartered in Grand Rapids, Michigan. When I first began my research, I did not think that it would result in a very large volume of work, but as I dug deeper into the subject, the pages began to pile up. Several friends graciously read my first rough drafts and suggested the possibility of having the manuscript published, which led to the work contained within these pages. I have innumerable people to thank, but I will try my best.

Timothy J. Todish of Grand Rapids, Michigan. Tim was, and continues to be my mentor when it comes to my writing projects. His patience and considerable knowledge of this subject were a godsend during the course of its writing.

Major John C. Jaeger of Flat Rock, Michigan. Without his vision all those years ago, none of this would have been possible.

Gary Zaboly of Bronx, New York. Gary's enthusiasm for the Rangers of the French and Indian War period, as well as Robert Rogers himself, is contagious. You cannot help but catch some of his passion for the subject when you correspond with him.

Tom Shisler of Maple Grove, Ohio. Tom took a raw Ranger recruit, and although I am still a project under construction, turned me into a reasonable rendition of a Ranger reenactor.

Christopher Matheney of Lancaster, Ohio. Chris has set the standard for the Ranger reenactors of our time with his portrayal of Robert Rogers in the History Channel series, "Legends of the Old Northwest."

Richard and JoAnne Fuller of Fort Edward, New York. They generously arranged for our unit to stay overnight on Rogers Island. Their personal tour of the island and extensive knowledge of the area was a high point of our stay.

Thomas Nesbitt from the Crown Point Historic Site, Crown Point, New York. A simple half-hour phone conversation with him led me to a couple of the maps used in this book. I appreciate the time he took from his busy day.

Christopher Fox, Curator of the Fort Ticonderoga Museum. His help finding a map I needed showing the location of the fortifications at Chambly and Isle aux Noix went beyond the call of duty.

The fine lads from the Ohio Company of Jaeger's Battalion. Terry Cochran, Brian Cohen, Rick Compton, Jim Henderly, Don Holsinger, Scott Hutcheson, Jeff Johnson, Phillip Jones, Darrel and Brian Lang, Bill McBroom, and Dan Reese. I have learned something from each one of them that ended up in this book.

All of the rest of Jaeger's Battalion, including Dan Schroth, Bill Blair, Randy Flood, Terry Todish and Dave Fagerberg. I would like to name all of them, but know that each one played a part in bringing this book to fruition.

Bill Hazelton, Editor of the *Journal of Jaeger's Battalion*, our group's quarterly newsletter. Thanks for letting me improve my writing skills, and putting up with my constant submissions.

Special thanks to Roxanne Carlson for her expert editing and formatting of this material. Without her guidance, I would have been lost in this sea of paperwork. Roxanne, you would have been able to command any of the scouts sent out under Major Rogers.

My parents, Gary and Sharon Wulff of Custar, Ohio. Their love of reading and of history led to my involvement in historical reenacting. Their constant support and guidance is appreciated more than they will ever know.

My daughter Brittany, who has endured many trips to historical sites over the years during family vacations. I am sure she has heard, "Just one more fort," more times than she cares to remember. One day I promise a vacation where we go anywhere but places that have "historical," or "fort" in the title.

My son Mike, who first took notice of those "soldiers in the green coats." His enthusiasm led to our joining Jaeger's Battalion, and the rest is history. He is a far better soldier than I will ever be.

Last, but certainly first, is my wife Beth. She is my biggest and constant supporter, as well as my best friend. She has endured my worst as well as my best during our years together. She forced me to learn to use a computer, and was very patient in fixing the hundreds of mistakes I made during the course of writing this book. She spent seemingly endless miles in the passenger seat while we drove to historical events. Beth, I would not have made the trip without you.

Preface

This book is a step-by-step analysis of Rogers' Rules, supported by historical references. Since this is a very specific look at a small part of the much larger conflict known as the "French and Indian War" in North America, a general knowledge of the conflict, and of Rogers Rangers will greatly assist the reader in the understanding of the Ranging Rules.

I would like to note that the rules discussed in this analysis are taken word for word directly from Robert Rogers' *Journals* of his exploits during the French and Indian War. A slightly more descriptive version of these rules exists, which was sent to British Commander in Chief Lord Loudoun, but the rules laid down in that text are the same as contained in Rogers' *Journals*. Rogers may have been trying to be more elegant in his formal presentation to Governor Shirley's replacement.

A version of Rogers Rules has been in circulation for many years, and has become widespread since the development of the Internet. The presence of this set of rules is sometimes confusing to historians or fans of the French and Indian War period in North America. I have even seen them listed in different publications as being the original set of rules that Rogers first wrote down in late 1757. This version is believed to have been written sometime in World War II, and again surfaced during the Vietnam War era. While you can see that these rules were developed from Rogers' original set of rules, they are clearly a modern version and should not be considered as Rogers' true Rules for the Ranging Service. Tim Todish, one of today's most knowledgeable historians on the subject of the Rangers, had this to say about this modern set of rules in *The Annotated and Illustrated Journals of Major Robert Rogers:*

> A document entitled *Standing Orders* for Rogers' Rangers that starts out "Don't forget nothing" has been circulating for years, and copies have been distributed to many modern army personnel. I have been able to trace this document back to the August 1962 issue of *True: The Man's Magazine.* Lieutenant Colonel John Lock, the author of the fine Ranger history *To Fight with Intrepidity. . .* has found

these same orders in a 1960 U.S. Army Ranger Training Manual. The folksy wording definitely has a foundation in the words of Sergeant McNott, a character in Kenneth Roberts' classic 1937 novel *Northwest Passage*. While they make for interesting reading, and do bear some resemblance to Rogers' real Ranging Rules, the *Standing Orders* are definitely a modern creation. (Todish/Zaboly, 79)

Noted author, artist and historian Gary Zaboly also adds these clues to the origin of this modern set of Ranging Rules in his biography of Robert Rogers, *A True Ranger: The Life and Many Wars of Major Robert Rogers:*

> Since World War II, in fact, Rogers' rules for ranging have been issued to Army Rangers, Green Berets, and other troops, and remain posted at Ranger battalion headquarters alongside the Ranger's creed. The school's *Ranger Handbook* lists "Standing Orders, Rogers' Rangers," on its fourth and fifth pages.
>
> Colonel David Hackworth issued Rogers' rules, printed on pocket-sized laminated cards, to his Infantry battalion in Vietnam. "These basics are the first things that soldiers forget – keeping your weapons clean, moving quietly, and so on," he notes. "If you can remember these simple rules, you can survive." (Zaboly, *A True Ranger*, 480)

When people come across this modern set of rules they need to remember that even though their basis can be traced back to "Robert Rogers' Rules for the Ranging Service," they are clearly a modern interpretation of the original French and Indian War set of rules. The only true set is that which Rogers himself put down on paper so many years ago.

Matt Wulff
Custar, Ohio
March 6, 2005

Robert Rogers' Rules or a Plan of Discipline for the Ranging Service

The first "ranging companies" in New England took up their muskets to help defend the frontier settlements from Indian raids in the seventeenth century. Many settlements hired or organized their own groups of "rangers" to patrol the surrounding areas and guard against attacks.

The men who became rangers were true woodsmen: hunters and trappers who could survive for long periods in the wilderness with only their firelocks and whatever they carried on their backs. They also understood the Indians' methods of fighting, giving just as well as they received.

Robert Rogers honed his frontier skills on the family farm near Rumford, New Hampshire. In 1746, at age fourteen, he joined a company of militia assigned to scout the Merrimack River Valley, his first taste of military duty. Rogers undoubtedly gained knowledge and experience from the older "Indian hunters" in the party. By the time of the "last" French and Indian War, these skilled woodsmen boasted reputations as expert shots with their flintlock muzzleloading firearms:

> The typical New Hampshire recruit could also "shoot amazingly well," as Captain Henry Pringle of the 27th Foot observed. Based at Fort Edward, and a volunteer in one of Rogers' biggest scouting excursions, Pringle wrote in December 1757 of one Ranger officer who, "the other day, at four shots with four balls, killed a brace of deer, a

pheasant, and a pair of wild ducks – the latter he killed at one shot." (Zaboly, *American Colonial Ranger*, 14)

Ranger companies scouted and gathered intelligence for the early Provincial regiments. Robert Rogers was the captain of the Ranger Company in Colonel Joseph Blanchard's New Hampshire Regiment in 1755 at the beginning of the French and Indian War. Under Provincial Major General William Johnson, Rogers and his company were part of the expedition against the French fort at Crown Point, in which the French, under Baron Dieskau, were defeated at the Battle of Lake George. Blanchard had introduced Major General Johnson to Rogers in a letter that recommended him, as state in Rogers' own words, as:

A person well acquainted with the haunts and passes of the enemy, and the Indian method of fighting. (Todish/ Zaboly, 36)

General Johnson needed good scouts and intelligence gatherers for his army, and he considered none better than Robert Rogers. Twelve years after the Crown Point expedition, Johnson said the following about Rogers in a letter to the Earl of Shelburne:

My Lord, This Gentleman has been known to me since 1755, when finding him an active man, I raised him to the Rank of a Provincial Officer and employed him on scouting service there being very few people then to be had fit for the purpose, he has since been advanced by several of the Commanders in Chief for his alertness in that way... (Hall, 6)

The early years of the French and Indian War were marked with disappointments and shattering losses for the British Army in America. The resounding defeat of General Braddock's Army at the Monongahela River, while on the way to strike the French at Fort Duquesne (modern day Pittsburgh, Pennsylvania), showed how unprepared the British Army was to wage warfare in the woodlands of America. British officers trained in European military tactics were ill-prepared for the guerrilla style of fighting practiced by the French and their Native American allies. The

British high command began to realize they must change their methods to meet this style of fighting.

The Duke of Cumberland, Massachusetts Governor William Shirley, and General William Johnson saw the need for Ranger companies. The Duke of Cumberland promoted as well the adaptation of Ranger tactics into the regular British regiments.

Rogers and his Ranger company had come to the attention of Shirley as a result of his service in the Crown Point campaign. Shirley was temporary Commander in Chief of the British forces in America in early 1756. Governor-General Shirley awarded Rogers command of an "Independent Company of Rangers" to consist of sixty private men and officers:

> According to the General's orders, my company was to consist of sixty privates, at 3s. New York currency per day, three searjents at 4s. an Ensign at 5s. a Lieutenant at 7s. and my own pay was fixed at 10s. per day. Ten Spanish dollars were allowed to each man towards providing cloaths, arms and blankets. My orders were to raise this company as soon as possible, to inlist none but such as were used to traveling and hunting, and in whose fidelity I could confide; they were, moreover to be subject to military discipline, and the articles of war. Our rendezvous was appointed at Albany, from thence to proceed in four whaleboats to Lake George, and, "From time to time, to use my best endeavours to distress the French and their allies, by sacking, burning, and destroying their houses, barns, barracks, canoes and battoes, &c. and by killing their cattle of every kind; and at all times to endeavour to way-lay, attack and destroy their convoys of provisions by land and water, in any part of the country where I could find them. (Rogers, *Journals*, 13)

Rogers' new command was on an independent establishment, which meant that his company of Rangers was not part of a permanent regiment in the British Army, and that he and his men would be paid and supplied or reimbursed by the Crown, as opposed to being paid and supplied by the provincial governments. Unfortunately, this also meant that his company could be disbanded at any time.

A second company under the command of Robert's brother Richard was established. Two other provincial Ranger companies under Captains Thomas Speakman and Humphrey Hobbs were also brought under Robert Rogers' leadership.

Rogers and his Rangers spent the next several months on scouting missions into enemy-held territory. The Rangers often carried out these scouts in the dead of winter, going on the offensive against the French when the rest of the British and Provincial Army were in their winter quarters.

During this time, Governor-General Shirley received his recall and temporarily was replaced by Major General Abercromby until the arrival of the new Commander in Chief of His Majesty's forces in America, John Campbell, the fourth Earl of Loudoun. Rogers updated Loudoun on the activities of the Rangers and was given the task of penetrating into the enemy's territory and burning their harvest, which was nearing full growth, and of otherwise distressing them. Rogers and his Rangers spent the rest of 1756 scouting and providing much valuable intelligence to the British Army.

The Rangers were making a name for themselves, sometimes good, and sometimes bad. While the work that the Rangers performed was deemed entirely necessary to the British cause, the Rangers often were thought of as a group of undisciplined ruffians, and many of the regular officers never had any respect for them. It must be remembered that there were at this time several companies of Rangers in operation on different fronts, and not all of them fell under Rogers' command. Rogers' companies were not exempt from criticism, though he himself generally was well regarded by regular and provincial officers alike.

The Duke of Cumberland, hearing of the problems of discipline among the Rangers, began to forward the idea of training regular troops in Ranger tactics. These specially trained regular troops would be able to fight and move in the ways of the Rangers, but with the discipline of regular troops, eventually becoming units of "light infantry." Lord Loudoun was also of this disposition, although he felt that until the regular troops could be trained, the Rangers were still badly needed:

On August 20, 1756, Loudoun wrote to the Duke of Cumberland: "From the Indians, you see we have no support; some Rangers I shall be obliged to keep all the winter, till I can make some of our own people fit for that service. When I arrived here, I found that there was a disposition in the Soldiers, to go out with Indians and Rangers, and that some of them were then out; I shall encourage it all I can, and if the parties that are out now, have success and escape, we shall soon get a knowledge of this country, and be able to March with much more safety than at present." (Todish/Zaboly, 56)

The Duke of Cumberland still pressed Loudoun for the augmentation and training of regular troops in the Ranger disciplines when he wrote to Loudoun on October 22, 1756:

"I hope that you will, in time, teach your troops to go out upon scouting parties: for, 'till *Regular* Officers with men that they can trust, learn to beat the woods, & to act as *Irregulars*, you never will gain any certain Intelligence of the enemy, as I fear, by this time you are convinced that Indian Intelligence & that of *Rangers* is not at all to be depended upon." (Todish/Zaboly, 56)

Loudoun knew that he had no choice but to comply with this pressure for reform from England, but still clung to the necessity of Rangers when he later wrote back to Cumberland:

I am afraid, I shall be blamed for the Ranging Companies; but as realy in effect we have no Indians, it is impossible for any Army to Act in this Country, without Rangers; and there ought to be a considerable body of them...for they will be able to deal with the Indians in their own way; and from all I can see, are much stronger and hardier fellows than the Indians.... (Todish/Zaboly, 57)

Rogers, as was customary for him, answered his critics in the only way he knew how, by taking his Rangers back into the woods on many new forays against the French in their own territory. During this period Lord George Augustus Howe, Brigadier General of the 55th Regiment of Foot, joined Rogers and his Rangers on one of their scouts:

...to learn our method of marching, ambushing, retreating, &c. and, upon our return, expressed his good opinion very generously. (Rogers, *Journals*, 51, 53)

Lord Loudoun gave orders to Rogers to take a group of volunteer officers from the regular troops and train them in the tactics of the Rangers so that they would be better able to fight and maneuver in the woods and brush. This group was formed together into what was known as the "cadet company":

About this time Lord Loudoun sent the following volunteers in the regular troops, to be trained to the ranging, or wood-service, under my command and inspection; with particular orders to me to instruct them to the utmost of my power in the ranging-discipline, our methods of marching, retreating, ambushing, fighting, &c. that they might be better qualified for any future services against the enemy we had to contend with, desiring me to take particular notice of each one's behavior, and recommend them according to their deserts... (Rogers, *Journals*, 52)

As noted earlier, Loudoun's real purpose was to eventually replace the Rangers eventually with specially trained Regular troops, led by Regular officers. This was partly due to the occasional difficulty in controlling and disciplining the American born and bred Ranger companies. The excessive cost of maintaining them was another factor. In 1758, nine Ranger companies cost twice as much as a full regiment of Regulars. (Anderson, pp.181 and 768-9 n.4) Nevertheless, it is clear that Loudoun deemed Rogers himself to be a very competent and valuable officer, and considered his Rangers to be among the best of the numerous Ranger units in the service. As time would show, for all their faults, the American Rangers never could be fully replaced by regular troops. (Todish/Zaboly, 71)

The volunteers were members of the 4th, 22nd, 27th, 42nd, 44th, 48th and 55th Regiments, as well as the 2nd, 3rd, and 4th Battalions of the Royal American Regiment. There were also some volunteers from some of the other provincial Ranger companies. Rogers took these men under his direct command and management, and to better help them learn the methods of the Rangers he wrote down the "Rules or a Plan of Discipline" that he felt necessary for the "Ranging Service." Tim Todish observes:

> Rogers' Ranging Rules are rightfully remembered as one of the first *written* manuals for irregular warfare in North America. However, Ranger tactics had been evolving here for many years. Benjamin Church, who fought in King Philip's War, 1675-76, practiced many of the same tactics used by Rogers, and his memoirs were published in Boston in 1716. Rogers certainly improved and perfected the concept, but he did not *invent* it, as others have sometimes claimed. (Todish/Zaboly, 78)

Rogers' Rules are twenty-eight instructions that he felt would best suit the Rangers, or the regulars acting as Rangers, in scouting and fighting in the deep forests of America:

> ...which on various occasions, I found by experience to be necessary and advantageous... (Rogers, *Journals*, 52)

Rogers' Rules:
Number One

All Rangers are subject to the rules and articles of war; to appear at roll-call every evening on their own parade, equipped, each with a firelock, sixty rounds of powder and ball, and a hatchet, at the same time an officer from each company is to inspect the same, to see they are in order, so as to be ready on any emergency to march at a minute's warning; and before they are dismissed, the necessary guards are to be draughted, and scouts for the next day appointed.

(Rogers, *Journals*, 55)

The first of Rogers' Rules laid down the groundwork for what was expected of the men under his command. With every new establishment of the Rangers, it was mandated that they be subject to the "Rules and Articles of War." We can get an idea of what this meant from the following orders given by General Abercromby in 1758:

> Whereas it may be of great use to his Majesties service in the operations now carrying on for recovering his rights in America, to have a number of men employed in obtaining intelligence of the strength, situation, and motions of the

enemy, as well as other services, for which Rangers, or men acquainted with the woods, only are fit: Having the greatest confidence in your loyalty, courage and skill in this kind of service, I do, by virtue of the power and authority given me by his Majesty, hereby constitute and appoint you to be Major of the Rangers in his Majesty's service, and likewise Captain of a company of said Rangers. You are therefore to take the said Rangers as Major, and said Company as Captain into your care and charge, and duly exercise and instruct, as well the officers as the soldiers thereof, in arms, and to use your best endeavors to keep them in good order and discipline; and I do hereby command them to obey you as their Major and Captain respectively, and you are to follow and observe such orders and directions from time to time as you shall receive from his Majesty, myself, or any other Superior officer, according to the rules and discipline of war. (Rogers, *Journals*, 93, 94)

The Rules and Articles of War are a set of regulations governing the behavior expected of the soldiers fighting for the British Army, Regulars and Provincials alike. They also stipulate the penalties for infractions. They are set in the following twenty sections:

Section 1: Divine worship. Deals with what is expected of the soldiers and officers when it comes to worship services and the penalties for breaking them.

Section 2: Mutiny. Deals with the penalties for disobedience to officers, disobeying orders and the like.

Section 3: Of enlisting soldiers. States the rules governing the enlistment of soldiers.

Section 4: Musters. Deals with furloughs, leaves and absences.

Section 5: Returns. Deals with troop returns.

Section 6: Desertion. Orders the penalties for desertion, being absent without leave and the like.

Section 7: Quarrels and sending challenges. Covers dueling, provoking arguments, and physical altercations.

Section 8: Suttling. Covers the rules and limits of persons or companies entitled to sell goods to the army.

Section 9: Quarters. Billeting or quartering of the troops other than in military barracks or installations.

Section 10: Carriages. Use of private carriages or other conveyances for the use of the army.

Section 11: Of crimes punishable by law. The matter of civil crimes committed by a member of the army against local laws or known laws of the land.

Section 12: Of redressing wrongs. What an officer or soldier must do if he thinks himself wronged.

Section 13: Of stores and ammunition. Selling of military stores without order, embezzlement, or damage by neglect.

Section 14: Of duties to quarters, in garrison and in the field. Soldiers being out of camp, missing parades, inspections, guard duty and the penalties for same.

Section 15: Administration of justice. Rules governing the administration of penalties following the proper rules, regulations and execution of court proceedings.

Section 16: Entry of commissions. Proper paperwork for commissions of officers.

Section 17: Half-pay. Officers at half pay are still under discipline and command as if under full pay.

Section 18: Effects of the dead. Deals with the disposal, distribution and care of a dead man's belongings.

Section 19: Artillery. Rules to be observed by officers and soldiers of the artillery train.

Section 20: Relating to the foregoing articles. States that the rules are to be read to the troops once in every two months and sets the precedent for and where a court martial can occur.

The penalties set in the above articles varied greatly but included loss of pay, court martial, reduction in rank, detention in irons or other confinement, or even death. Many soldiers of the day, including the Rangers, enlisted as much for advancement, as for patriotic reasons. The loss of pay and rank, not to mention the very real threat of death, would have been a real deterrent to breaking these rules.

While we may never know for sure the true extent to which the Rangers adhered to the Rules and Articles of War, we do know that the rules were read to the Rangers, they were part of their establishments as Independent Companies, and the Rangers were expected to act in accordance with them. We also know that the Rangers were not always the most disciplined troops.

These rules were not simply read to the regular soldiers and then forgotten. Throughout the war, these rules were the basis of conduct of the soldiers fighting for the British Army. References to infractions of the rules and the punishments doled out filled the orderly books and journals of the war:

> On July 10, ten waggoners of the provincials were tried for stealing his majesty's arms and working-tools; one was sentenced to receive four hundred lashes, the others three hundred each: the general made a public example of the principle, by ordering him first to be punished at the head of every regiment, and then to be turned out of camp and deemed unworthy to serve in the army; the other delinquents his excellency was pleased to pardon, but ordered that they should be marched prisoners to see the punishment inflicted on the chief transgressor. (Knox, *Siege of Quebec*, 164)

Four hundred lashes would have been terrible, but to endure them in front of their friends and fellow soldiers would have doubled the pain for many of His Majesty's soldiers.

When Rogers ordered the Rangers to "appear at roll call every evening on their own parade," we know that he wanted a roll call of the Ranger companies to make sure everyone was accounted for and that no one was missing without leave; but what does he mean by, "on their own parade"? The Funk and Wagnall's standard desk dictionary defines a parade ground as "a ground where military reviews are held." The Regular army used the parade ground to practice or display their proficiency in their standard military drill.

> I flattered myself I should have seen the grenadier companies of this garrison reviewed by General Wolfe, but it was over before I could get there; I was told they went through all their manoevres and evolutions with great exactness and spirit, according to the new system of discipline. (Knox, *Siege of Quebec*, 117)

Eighteenth-century military encampments usually were tent camps set up within defensive works that had been built—or "thrown up"—by the soldiers. Tent camps also were set up within the outer defenses of fortifications such as Forts Edward and William Henry. The amount of barracks space at these forts could not hold the numbers of troops often assigned to them. The tent encampments were laid out according to the rules of "Military Castrametation" as set up in Humphrey Bland's 1759 *Treatise of Military Discipline,* which states the:

> General rules for the encamping of an Army, with the particulars for the Regiment of horse, and a Battalion of foot; and two plans of the same. (Bland, Chapter 17, 285)

These rules specified, on a large scale, the way that the tent camps were to be set up. The design began with the tents of the non-commissioned officers, then the private men, in company rows. Precise measurements between the tent rows created company streets. The officers' tents followed, starting with the subalterns on up to the regiment's colonel. The plan also designated locations for kitchen areas and sutlers' tents.

Regiments were arranged as they would be deployed in battle. Large open areas were set aside as parade grounds. The painting, "View of the Lines at Lake George 1759," by Captain Thomas Davies, very clearly shows the tent lines of the British Army preparing for the 1759 campaign against Ticonderoga. This painting is in the Fort Ticonderoga museum.

The Rangers, however, did not care for the tent encampments. They were experts at building small bark shelters for temporary camps, evidence of their extreme dislike of tents:

> Tents were anathema to all Rangers; they preferred to live in even half-faced camps of brush rather than tents like the rest of the army. (Todish/Zaboly, 82)

If the Rangers were to be encamped for a long period, such as at the Ranger camp on Rogers' Island in the Hudson River across from Fort Edward, they preferred to build log huts to live in:

> The Rangers, with the before mentioned volunteers were encamped and quartered in huts on an adjacent island in the Hudson River, and were sent out on various scouts. (Stott/Mason, 8)

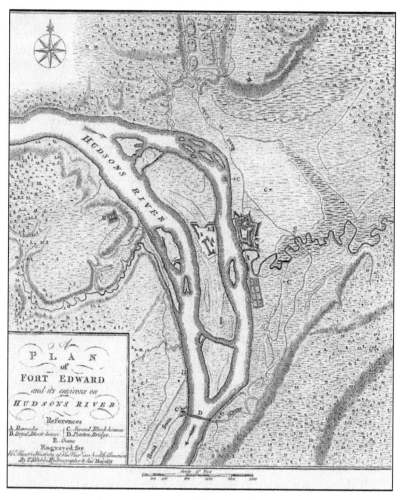

Figure 1. This is a map showing the Fort Edward, Rogers Island area as it appeared in 1759. The Rangers' huts are believed to have been in the area just to the south of the barracks, marked "A" on the map. This map is from Thomas Mante's *History of the Late War in North America* (London 1772).

The Rangers preferred these smaller shelters as opposed to barracks, as they were much easier to keep warm.

> Dividing the waters of the Hudson in front of the fort (Edward) is Rogers Island, a beautiful and romantic spot.... Almost every year the plow turns up some curious relics of the past upon the island, such as bayonets, tomahawks, buttons, bullets, cannonballs, coin, arrowheads, etc. (Stott, 24)

Archeological excavations on the island in 1960 by landowner Earl Stott found the remains of two hut rows, twenty feet on center, separated by company streets. The outlines of brick fireplaces were found in the remains of the hut sites.

Another painting by Captain Davies, "A South View of the New Fortress at Crown Point...in the Year 1759," shows the rows of huts built by the Rangers. These huts appear to be made of horizontal logs, with peaked roofs, and sharing a common wall with the next hut in the row. They are set up with streets between them, much like the company streets in a tent encampment. There is also a large open area in front of the huts that may have been the Rangers' parade ground. When Rogers ordered his men to appear at roll call each evening on their own parade, we can assume that he wanted his Rangers to establish their own area for drill and review adjacent to their encampments.

Does this mean that the Rangers practiced and performed the same drill as the Regular troops? There are no known references to the Rangers practicing the "Manual Exercise" as set forth in Bland's manual, but we can assume that the Rangers were at least knowledgeable of the standard military drill and would have practiced it. The establishment of separate parade grounds in their camps lends some credibility to this theory. We also know that the Rangers sometimes marched and fought in conjunction with Regular troops. The advance against Ticonderoga in 1759, when Rogers Rangers made up part of the advanced guard of the British Army, is one example:

> Like the rest of the army on this day, the advanced guard marches in two columns, each two ranks wide. The Rangers under Major Robert Rogers comprise one column, and

Gage's Light Infantry (the 80th) the other. (Todish/ Zaboly, 163)

Even though the members of the 80th on this march were light infantrymen, they were still Regulars, and the Rangers must have had at least a general knowledge of marching and maneuvering in the manner of the Regulars in order to sustain an orderly march. The amount of time spent working with the Regular army, especially later in the war, would also support the idea that the Rangers, while not as proficient as Regulars, would have had a working knowledge of their drill.

We must remember that since we have no concrete evidence to support or refute the idea of the Rangers practicing the Regulars' manual exercise, the references stated above are in support of assumptions that we are making concerning the Rangers and military drill. Hopefully one day we may find the historical facts needed to confirm or deny the use of the British Army manual exercise by the Rangers.

When the Rangers fell in for roll call, Rogers expected them to be fully equipped with a firelock, sixty rounds of powder and ball, and a hatchet. A description of the Rangers by Captain John Knox gives one of our best ideas of what a Ranger looked like early in the French and Indian War:

> A body of rangers, under the command of Captain Rogers, who arrived with the other troops from the southward, march out everyday to scour the country; these light troops have, at present, no particular uniform, only they wear their cloaths short, and are armed with a firelock, tomahock or small hatchet, and a scalping knife; a bullocks horn full of powder hangs under their right arm, by a belt from the left shoulder; and a leathern or seals skin bag, buckled round their waist, which hangs down before, contains bullets and a smaller shot of the size of full-grown peas: six or seven of which, with a ball, they generally load; and their officers usually carry a small compass fixed in the bottoms of their powder-horns, by which to direct them when they happen to lose themselves in the woods. (Knox, *Siege of Quebec*, 22)

The firelocks used by the Rangers would have been any number of different kinds of weapons. When the Rangers were first established, they were not issued arms; instead, they were given money towards providing their own arms:

> Ten Spanish dollars were allowed each man towards providing cloaths, arms, and blankets. (Rogers, *Journals*, 13)

Many of the early Rangers, being expert hunters as stated before, would have brought their own hunting weapons with them. They would have been more comfortable with the arms that helped to feed their families and friends on the frontier. Some may have bought arms from the British Army if they were available, but many were paid an additional bounty if they provided their own arms and they were certified as serviceable by the army. Archeological investigations on Rogers Island and the site of Fort Edward attest to the variety of arms in use:

> British army sites are denoted by the .75 cal. Musket balls for Brown Besses, while early ranger or provincial sites contain balls of .48 to .69 calibre. (Stott, 28)

Rogers may have used his personal firelock early in the war on a scout to the French fort at Crown Point, Fort St. Frederick:

> About ten o'clock a single man marched out directly towards our ambush. When I perceived him within ten yards of me, I sprung over the log, and met him, and offered him quarters, which he refused, and made a pass at me with a dirk, which I avoided, and presented my fusee to his breast; but notwithstanding, he still pushed with resolution, and obliged me to dispatch him. (Rogers, *Journals*, 5)

The Rangers were also to be equipped with sixty rounds of powder and ball. This is an above average amount of ammunition for the French and Indian War soldier. Rogers and his men could expect to be out in the woods scouting for several days at a time, during which they would be unsupported by any means of supply from the army. This extra ammunition allowed them to function without regard to supply. The Rangers were also known for the constant fire that they were able to give their enemy. They also would fire and reload on their own, or independent of commands from an officer. They would have needed a larger amount of ammunition to sustain themselves due to their tactics and methods.

Regular troops normally were issued eighteen, twenty-four, or thirty-six cartridges at a time. This was about half, or even less than half the amount the Rangers usually carried:

> The troops are ordered to be completed to 36 rounds of good cartridges, with three flints per man, and to be in readiness to land at the shortest notice. (Knox, *Siege of Quebec*, 272)

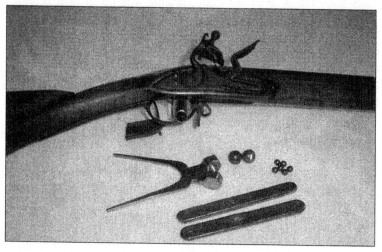

Figure 2. An early light fusil of .62 caliber, along with some round ball, smaller shot the size of "full-grown peas," and a brass bullet mold for casting balls.

The mention of "good cartridges" in this quote illustrates the difference between the way the Regulars and the Rangers carried their ammunition. The earlier description by Knox states that the Rangers carried a "bullocks horn full of powder" and a small "leathern or seals skin bag," for carrying their ball and buckshot. By carrying their powder in powder horns, they were able to keep their powder dry, as opposed to paper cartridges carried by Regular troops that were susceptible to damage from the weather. An example of this was during the attempted landing at "Point a Lessay" during the 1759 siege of Quebec. The first division of the troops, consisting of all the grenadiers of the army, had to abort the landing due to confusion in the formations, and a rainstorm:

The general, seeing the situation of affairs, night drawing on a-pace and the ammunition of the army damaged with the dreadfullest thunder-storm and fall of rain that can be conceived, sent to stop Brigadier Townsend, and ordered Brigadier Monckton to reimbark his division and the scattered corps of grenadiers in the best manner he could. (Knox, *Siege of Quebec*, 157)

Powder horns are containers made from the horns of a cow. The horn is hollowed out and then a wooden plug is made to fit the open end, sealing it against moisture. The other end is then shaped into a spout and fitted with a wooden stopper. Black powder is then stored inside the horn and poured out in measured amounts in order to "charge" the firelock.

Most of the Rangers made their own powder horns, but sometimes they obtained them from manufacturers or skilled craftsmen. The leather or sealskin ammunition bags that the Rangers wore on a belt in front of their bodies provided easy access to the round ball and buckshot carried inside. This way of carrying ammunition leads us to believe that the Rangers preferred to load from loose powder and ball, instead of paper cartridges as the Regulars did.

There is a reference to the use of a paper cartridge during a scout by the Rangers. Captain Henry Pringle of the 27th Regiment was a volunteer on the scout that led to the "Battle on Snowshoes" on March 13, 1758. After the battle and near annihilation of his command, Rogers and the survivors of the battle crept away when it became dark, traveling separately or in small groups back to Lake George, where they had hidden their hand sleys. Captain Pringle and another volunteer became separated and lost during this retreat due to problems with their snowshoes. They spent the next several days barely existing in the harsh and miserably cold weather until French soldiers captured them. During their ordeal in the woods, they tried to start a fire to warm themselves:

"If we halted a minute we became pillars of ice; so that we were resolved, as it froze so hard, to make a fire, although the danger was apparent. Accidentally we had one dry cartridge, and in trying with my pistol if it would flash a little of the powder, Mr. ------- unfortunately held the cartridge too near, by which it took fire, blew up in our faces, almost blinded him, and gave excessive pain." (Rogers, *Journals*, 89, 90)

Captain Pringle was of course a Regular soldier, and would have been accustomed to the use of paper cartridges, so this does not help us determine if the Rangers used them. We also know that the companies under Hobbs and Speakman were issued cartridge boxes with straps. These two companies were already established before being brought under the command of Robert Rogers, so this is probably not a concrete example of the Rangers using cartridge boxes as opposed to powder horns and shot bags. Two references from Orderly Books from Fort Edward attest to the use of loose powder and ball by the Rangers:

A return of ye two Ranging company's to be given in immediately to ye commanding offr making mention of ye condition of their arms, Powder horns, shot bags and tomahawks. (Pray, 9)

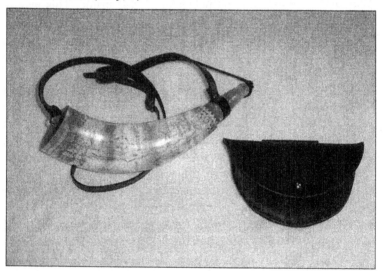

Figure 3. A reproduction French and Indian War era engraved powder horn, which holds about a pound of powder, with its leather sling. The leather belt bag carries round ball and buckshot.

And again at Fort Edward, July 5, 1757:

> The commanding officers of ye different regts to send to Mr. Furnis contractor of ye Ordnance.... To receive their Damaged Cartridges and Spair Bullets, for which he will give a recait. The men belonging to ye Provincial regt who are appointed to do ye duty of Rangers are to be emmediately supplied with leather shot bags and powder horns to carry ammunition. (Pray, 9)

The Rangers were known for loading a combination of small buckshot and regular-sized musket balls, or what was known as "buck and ball." Another reference talks about the method of breaking up issued paper cartridges if the soldier did not have a cartridge box, and the placing the powder in their powder horns:

> Albany May 31st 1759. Those that have not cartridge boxes must break their cartridges and put their powder into horns. (Pray, 9)

Due to the many different calibers of firelocks used by the Rangers, whether personal weapons or issued firearms, many of the Rangers would have had to cast their own round ball and buckshot, using pure lead and a bullet mold. As stated before, excavations on Rogers Island have turned up many different sizes of musket balls, but these diggings also uncovered lead casting sprue, the leftover remains of the casting procedure. One of the areas excavated is thought to be a shop area, due to the artifacts found there, including many axes of different sizes and whetstones:

> Musket balls and lead casting sprue were numerous at this site, and a cache of 67 balls of .59 to .60 calibre along with swan shot was found. Four balls that were excavated at this shop area turned out to be made of a hard glaze pottery instead of lead. Micrometer readings showed these balls to be within 2 thousandths of an inch of being perfect spheres. It is possible that these unusual balls were used in checking gun barrel calibers or as patterns for making bullet molds. (Stott, 24)

These .59 or .60 caliber bullets are of the size normally used in the hunting fusils of the day, and the presence of casting sprue proves that some of the men were indeed casting their own ammunition.

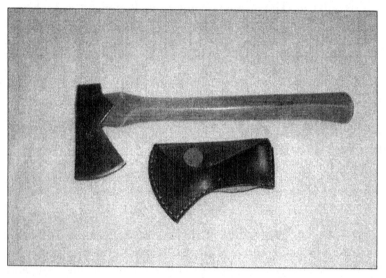

Figure 4. A common belt axe or hatchet with a hammer poll. A multi-purpose tool like the hatchet fits the methods of the Rangers in its versatility.

The discovery of many different kinds of axes brings us to another important piece of the Rangers gear as mentioned in Rule Number One, the hatchet. The excerpt from Knox also mentions the Rangers using a tomahawk or small hatchet. These weapons and tools were very familiar to the New Hampshire frontiersman. Tomahawk use by Native Americans is well documented, even back to the flint and stone weapons they made before steel axes became available from European traders. Many of the Rangers who used a belt axe as their personal weapon would have carried one in place of the Regular's bayonet. A hatchet was also easier to use in the woods and brush, as opposed to a long bayonet on the end of a musket. A hatchet had many other uses besides as a weapon. Most hatchets had a flat or hammer poll on the end opposite the cutting edge, enabling it to be used like a hammer. Hatchets were also used for cutting wood, butchering animals or game, and squaring off wood for frames or planking. The Rangers would have used them in the construction of the bark shelters they are known to have built, or even for something as simple as breaking up their "ships bread," the hard biscuits that were issued at times with their food rations. The hatchet's main purpose, though, was that of a weapon. The following quote from Private Thomas Brown shows how a hatchet might have been used:

> Brown "retir'd into the rear, to the prisoner I had taken on the lake, Knock'd him on the head, and killed him, lest he should Escape and give Information to the enemy." (Zaboly, *American Colonial Ranger*, 47)

Rogers also required that his Rangers always be ready to march at a moment's notice. This meant that they had to have their arms, weapons, and gear prepared so they could travel at the first warning. A Ranger had to carry enough provisions to sustain him for what could be several days on the trail with no chance for resupply. He also had to carry his required amount of ammunition. His firelock must be in good order and his hatchet sharp and ready for use. A Ranger would be able to travel as lightly as possible, but still be prepared for anything the French, or nature, could throw at him.

The weather played an important role in a Ranger's choice of gear and clothing. Heavy snow required snowshoes, ice creepers, and maybe even ice skates on which to travel. The Rangers made use of these items to enable them to carry the war into French territory, even in the dead of winter. The following quote from Colonel Beamsley Glazier of the New York Provincials shows the concern for carrying out winter warfare:

> "You are to take Good Care of your men and not Expose them too much you are to use all Immaginable Protection not to Loos a man if it should Snow you are to Return Imedintly to this Fort…" (Todish/Zaboly, 42)

Rogers's *Journals* are filled with references to the amount of snow and the slow travel that it caused. Snowshoes greatly aided the Rangers when traveling overland. The Rangers were skilled in the use and manufacture of snowshoes, as supported by the following quote from Rogers himself:

January 15, 1757. Agreeable to orders from the commanding officer at Fort Edward, I this day marched with my own Lieutenant Mr. Stark, Ensign Richard Page of Captain Richard Rogers Company, and fifty privates of said companies to Fort William Henry, where we were employed in providing provisions, snowshoes, &c. till the 17th. (Rogers, *Journals*, 35)

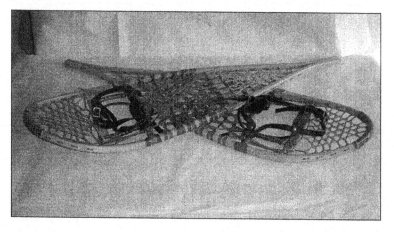

Figure 5.   A typical pair of wooden snowshoes. The rounded front and tapered tail is a quite common design from the eighteenth century.

Snowshoes enable the user to distribute his weight over a larger area, preventing him from sinking into deep snow. They are made from bent forms of wood and rawhide webbing with leather harnesses or ties to attach them to the feet as shown in the photo. Snowshoe use was quite common by the Native Americans and hunters on the frontier.

Rangers wearing snowshoes were sent out to pack down the trails that were then used by Regular and Provincial soldiers who were not trained in the use of snowshoes.

The commanding Officers of regiments are desired to make their light infantry practise walking on snow-shoes, preparatory to the service for which they are reserved; to this end five pair of these rackets are delivered to each corps, and the Officers of the light-armed companies are to be answerable that they are neither lost nor broken: some of

Captain Hazen's New-England Rangers are appointed to instruct our soldiers in the use of them. (Knox, *Historical Journal*, vol. II, 312)

The deep snow in the areas of Lake Champlain and Lake George made travel nearly impossible, as related in a letter written by Captain Henry Pringle of the 27th Regiment, a volunteer with Rogers at the Battle of Rogers Rock:

Before morning we contrived with forked sticks and strings of leather, a sort of snowshoes to prevent sinking entirely...

And later in the same letter:

Our snowshoes breaking, and sinking to our middle every fifty paces... (Todish/ Zaboly, 105)

We begin to get the feel for the difficulties of traveling in deep snow and the use of snowshoes by the Rangers to overcome these problems. The French and their native allies were known to attack patrols of soldiers on packed trails, driving them into deep snow, where they were easily captured or killed by their snowshoe-wearing attackers.

Moccasins were the preferred footwear when using snowshoes. The standard military or civilian shoe of the eighteenth century was ill-suited for the rough terrain of the forests. Many shoes would literally fall apart after just a few days' use. The Rangers, many of them raised on the frontier, literally living in the woods, adopted the use of moccasins or "Indian shoes." This easily-made leather footwear required patching almost on a daily basis, but it was far better for the woods than the typical colonial shoe of the day. Moccasins were also better suited for use in the winter than shoes, providing more warmth and protecting the foot better. This is confirmed by an unfortunate incident that befell a group of Regulars and Rangers that left Crown Point on a trip to Ticonderoga in December of 1759:

On December 25, A British Captain led 100 grumbling Regulars and Rangers from Crown Point to Ticonderoga to bring back the new clothing. Instead of ordering all men to wear moccasins and socks, which would have minimized the chance of frostbite, he allowed the greater part of them to march in regulation shoes. As a consequence all of the Rangers and Privates who wore shoes were frostbitten and the Surgeon at Crown Point had to cut off more than 100 frozen toes. (Loescher, vol. II, 70)

Figure 6. Reproduction leather moccasins of the type used by Rogers and his Rangers. An extra sole or "footing" of heavy leather has been sewn to the bottom of the moccasins.

Figure 7. Reproduction colonial military shoes. They are made on a straight last, which means that there is not a right or left shoe. You can see how these shoes would not be sensible for use in the snow.

Figure 8. These leather shoepack moccasins are fitted with a heavy wool blanket liner for use with snowshoes in heavy snow and cold weather.

Weight distribution when traveling over snow and ice can be a cause for great concern. Traveling across the ice was one of the easiest ways to travel in winter when deep snow made marching difficult, but it also had its inherent dangers. Thin ice was a common problem when traveling on the frozen lakes and streams. Rogers himself relates this danger with the following entries in his journals:

> We then attempted to cross the lake, but found the ice too weak. (Rogers, *Journals*, 11)

> I then called in the advanced guard, and flanking party, and marched on to the west shore, where in a thicket, we hid our sleys and packs. (Rogers, *Journals*, 75)

The use of small hand sleighs, or "sleys," enabled the Rangers to travel quickly over the frozen terrain. After the Second Battle on Snowshoes, The Rangers rendezvoused where they had hidden their sleys on Lake George and used the sleys to transport those unable to march to Hoop Island. There they met with Captain Stark, who had been sent by Colonel Haviland to assist the party in bringing in their wounded. Historian Gary Zaboly offers the following description of a typical Indian toboggan:

An Indian toboggan, varying in length from 6 to 12 ft, usually made of two planks of green spruce, birch, or elm wood that were lashed together with rawhide. The front of the sled was rolled back and held with guy ropes to the main body. Rawhide lines or ropes drew the toboggan, which could haul supplies and other heavy loads over deep snow. Sometimes a tumpline was used to draw it; on occasions dogs were employed, much like huskies. (Zaboly, *American Colonial Ranger*, 56)

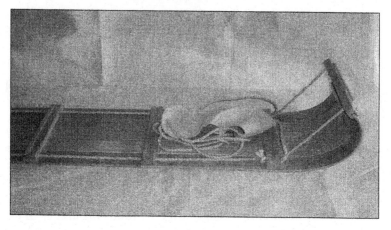

Figure 9. A small wooden sley of the size that could be used by one or two men.

The Rangers frequently strapped on their ice creepers for better traction over the icy terrain, and on rivers and lakes. Ice creepers were metal bars with four spikes or teeth that extended down to grab into the ice surface. They were worn on the instep of the foot and attached with leather straps or thongs as shown in the accompanying photo of a recreated pair. British Captain John Knox gives an excellent description of ice creepers in his journals:

Creepers, which are an invention calculated for the hollow of the foot, that buckles on like a spur, it is a small plate of iron an inch broad, with two ears that come up on both sides of the shoe between the ancle and the instep, with a stud on each of them, for eh leathers: from the two extremities are four stout points turned downward for two thirds of an inch, which, by the weight of the person who wears them, are indented in the ice. This contrivance is actually necessary, and prevents many fatal accidents. (Knox, *Historical Journal*, vol. I, 134)

Figure 10. A pair of reproduction ice creepers.

Ice creepers have been found at many French and Indian War sites, including Rogers Island. A good picture of the ice creepers found on Rogers Island is included in the publication *Exploring Rogers Island*, published in 1969 by the Rogers Island Historical Association, Fort Edward, New York.

Another unique way that the Rangers conducted raids up the frozen lakes, was upon ice skates. The following quote from Rogers' *Journals* supports their use by his Rangers:

January 14, 1756. I this day marched with a party of seventeen men, to reconnoiter the French forts, we proceeded down the lake, on the ice, upon skaits, and halted for refreshments near the fall out of Lake George into Lake Champlain. (Rogers, *Journals*, 10)

Most early ice skates consisted of a wooden platform for the foot, and a metal blade attached to the bottom of the wood. Again, leather straps or thongs attached it to the foot. The ability to make and to use these simple pieces of equipment, to carry the war into the heart of the enemy's territory, is typical of the Rangers' resourcefulness.

Figure 11. A pair of recreated ice skates that were adapted from the illustration of Ranger uniforms in *The Annotated and Illustrated Journals of Major Robert Rogers* by noted artist and historian Gary Zaboly.

A blacksmith would have hand-forged the metal ice creepers and the metal parts of the ice skates. Ice skates were also used for pleasure, with even the officers of the British Army using them in this manner, skating on the ice of the frozen marshes near Fort Cumberland, in Nova Scotia:

> Our principle amusement here is skating; the marshes, having been overflowed before the frost set in, afford us now a scope of several miles. (Knox, *Siege of Quebec*, 98)

Frigid cold required clothing that kept the Rangers warm, but allowed mobility. One of the ways a Ranger could pack light in cold weather and still stay warm was to use his blanket as a "matchcoat." By draping his blanket over his shoulders and belting it at his waist, he could fashion a cloak. It is believed that several of Rogers' men were wearing their blankets in this manner on March 7, 1759, when they ambushed a French detail out cutting wood near Lake Champlain:

Before they swooped down on the woodcutters, Rogers
notes, both he and his men "stripped off our blankets," an
indication that the Rangers probably wore their blankets
matchcoat-fashion, like the Indians, or like cloaks.
(Todish/Zaboly, 152)

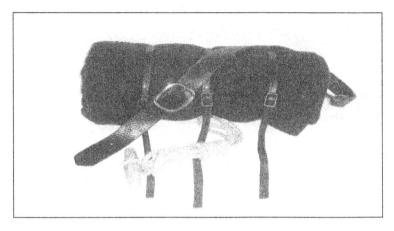

Figure 12. Blanket rolled and secured with a wide adjustable leather belt,
or "tumpline," by which it was carried.

Many of the Rangers, accustomed to the hardships of the
frontier winters, were familiar with this method of using their
blankets. The Rangers also wore blanket coats during their winter
scouts. These coats were made from old blankets, or blanket
material. They were crudely fashioned, but easily made, and very
warm. Many of the army's sutlers carried these coats for sale to
the soldiers. Rogers purchased blanket coats for his men as an
"enticement" on the mission to accept the surrender of the western
French-held outposts after the end of the war:

> Blanket coats, to the number of 170 had been purchased
> from Cole for the detachment, being a gratuity to the
> soldiers to encourage them to cross the lakes. (Loescher,
> vol. II, 131)

Greatcoats or watch coats were worn as well. These heavy
overcoats, made of coarse, nappy wool, were well suited for
traveling in the winter or for keeping warm while on sentry duty.

Such overcoats were not new to them, when one is reminded of the "19 great coats" issued to Rogers men in December of 1755. (Todish/Zaboly, 305)

Another way of always being prepared to "march at a moment's warning," was the ability to make quick decisions. The perpetual need for intelligence of the enemy's positions and designs to attack the British Army kept the Rangers out on scouts almost constantly, requiring them to be ready to travel at any time, especially early in the war. William Johnson and Governor Shirley were well aware of the need for this information:

> Johnson badly needed to know what was going on beyond the blank wall of forested mountains separating him from the French and their Indian Allies. Rumor and fear were killing the will of the army to push on. Without intelligence he had no answer to Shirley, now commander in chief, who refused to believe reports of French strength. At this critical point, Johnson's trusted scouts, the Mohawks, deserted him. With assurances that it was their intention to return, they departed on 11 September. Their intention soon changed; not only did they fail to return, but they turned back other Indians they encountered on the way. Desperate, Johnson inquired of the New Hampshire regiment—now at Lake George—for men of scouting ability. Colonel Blanchard recommended Robert Rogers, who reported to the General. (Cuneo, 21)

The speed at which the Rangers, and Rogers in particular, could react to a situation was well known and well deserved. After the capture of the small French fortification of St. Therese in early 1760, Rogers was faced with the possibility of being cut off by the French forces stationed at Isle aux Noix. He reacted in his typical, straightforward manner:

> Rogers learned that some young men had slipped through the ranger net and fled towards Fort Chambly. The countryside would be aroused. Rogers moved fast: women and children were sent towards Montreal; the fort and houses were fired; wagons, provisions, cattle, and boats were destroyed–except for eight used to transport the

rangers and twenty-six male prisoners to the east bank of the river. Now Rogers turned southerly. He tried to give Isle aux Noix a wide berth, but the French were waiting for him. His advance guard fell in the van of eight hundred French, but the main body failed to back up its advanced party. (Cuneo, 124)

Rogers continued his march, and due to his quick action, he and his command were able to escape to the safety of some boats he had waiting for his return. He and the rest of his party had just embarked when the enemy appeared on the shore behind them. Rogers had thought ahead, having the ships' commanders cruise their boats nearby, just in case the Rangers would have to escape very quickly by water. This forethought prevented his command from being trapped between the water and the enemy. Rogers always seemed to be thinking two or three steps ahead of the enemy, and his men learned this lesson well.

Rogers also wanted his officers to establish the men assigned to scouting missions for the next day, and the drafting of the proper guards for the camp at the evening roll call.

One thing that a person soon learns when studying Robert Rogers is that he always wanted his men to be on guard against being surprised. Guards were needed for the safety of the Rangers' camp. By always being alert, the Rangers were often able to turn what could have been a disaster into another Ranger triumph. Many of the Rangers' scouting missions were conducted at night, when the darkness helped to hide their movements. This was the case whether traveling by land or upon the many lakes and streams in the area. Once again, by constantly being ready with all weapons and gear, and their assignments taken care of ahead of time, the Rangers would often be many miles down the trail before the rest of the army was even stirring.

Figure 13. The author, dressed in the winter clothing of a typical eighteenth-century Ranger: on snowshoes, wearing winter moccasins, coarse woolen leggings, gray wool blanket coat, and wool mittens made from scrap blanket wool. His ammunition is carried in a small leather or "sealskin bag" which hangs on a belt in front of him.

This ends our analysis of Rogers' Rule Number One. We learned what Rogers expected of his men as to their discipline and personal conduct. The Rangers were held to the same rules and regulations as the Regular troops. Rogers was very specific as to the weapons and gear he expected the men to carry. The Rangers were an independent group of men who would rather live in half-faced bark shelters than tents. They could be rapidly deployed against the enemy due to their ability to react quickly and march at a minute's warning when called upon. Many of the Rangers were expert shots and seasoned hunters, just as at home in the deep, uncharted woods as they were on their frontier farms. The Rangers could travel in all kinds of weather over all kinds of country, often unmapped, with nothing but a compass or their own woods skills to guide them. If the Rangers were unable to be supplied by the army, they could feed themselves from what they could find or hunt out on the trail. The Rangers were well suited to the rigors of traveling in the dead of winter, which enabled them to continue the fight against the French when the rest of the army went into winter quarters. Their use of snowshoes, ice skates and other items suited for winter travel was a Ranger trademark.

Rogers' Rules: Number Two

Whenever you are ordered out to the enemies forts or frontiers for discoveries, if your numbers be small, march in a single file, keeping at such distance as to prevent one shot from killing two men, sending one man, or more, forward, and the like on each side, at the distance of twenty yards from the main body, if the ground you march over will admit of it, to give the signal to the officer of the approach of an enemy, and of their number, &c.

(Rogers, *Journals*, 55)

At the beginning of the series of French and Indian wars, the British Army had to adapt to a different style of warfare being waged in the vast forests of the new world, as opposed to the European style of warfare that took place on open battle fields. This forest warfare required different tactics and methods than the formal European style of battle.

We have already learned that the Rangers were unequaled when it came to scouting the enemy's forts and in gaining much needed intelligence of their plans and strategies against the British Army. Thomas Mante is attributed with the following quote about one early scout of Robert Rogers:

Whilst preparations were making on both sides for the next campaign, Captain Robert Rogers, on that of the English, was constantly employed in patroling the woods about the Forts Edward and William-Henry, and observing the motions of the French at Ticonderoga and Crown Point; that this service he performed with so much alertness, that he made a great number of prisoners, and thereby procured very good intelligence of the enemy. (Todish/Zaboly, 41)

On these scouts, Rogers' rule was to march in a single or "Indian" file, especially when traveling in small groups. Rogers and the Rangers conducted these scouts against an enemy that was ever vigilant against attack, just as the Rangers were. The French and their native allies kept patrols out constantly, trying to catch the Ranger patrols. The French were well aware of these intelligence-gathering scouts. Captain Louis-Antoine Bougainville remarked on these scouts in a journal entry:

They [the British] have little parties of Scottish Highlanders and a few Indians continually observing from the heights and the woods that surround Carillon. I suspect that they have established a flying camp behind the mountains north of the lake which supplies and shelters all these little parties. (Todish/Zaboly, 53)

These parties of "Scottish Highlanders" were most likely groups of Rangers on scouting and spying missions. The French would soon learn of Robert Rogers and his Rangers.

Because the French knew of these patrols and had their own parties out on scouting missions, getting through the area undetected was critical for the safety of these small Ranger units. By traveling in single file formation, they could penetrate the enemy's territory without being seen or tracked. They could minimize the disturbance to the surrounding area, lessening the chance it would be detected by a roving French patrol. They also could melt invisibly into the underbrush in the event of coming across one of the enemy's scouts. The lead Ranger in the formation could pick the route in front of him that would leave the least amount of tracks, while navigating around difficult terrain.

Rogers was specific about the distance he wanted his men to maintain between each other. By spreading out, they made a more difficult target if discovered by the enemy. We have already learned what crack shots the Rangers were, and we know they practiced shooting at marks whenever possible. The Rangers practiced so much that Lieutenant Colonel Haviland, in command at Fort Edward, complained about the Rangers' use of ammunition:

> Rogers instructed his companies to practice firing at marks so frequently that at least one British commander, Lieutenant-Colonel William Haviland scolded him, considering it an "extravagance in Ammunition." (Zaboly, *American Colonial Ranger*, 56)

Earlier, in Rule Number One, we saw a reference to a Ranger killing two wild ducks with one ball. Two men, standing too close together, would make a far larger and easier target to hit than two small ducks. Seemingly amazing feats of marksmanship were quite common on the frontier, where the ability to shoot straight could mean the difference between living and dying, or starving to death. At Cherry Pond on the New Hampshire frontier, hunter Dennis Stanley performed one of these feats:

> Fast loading by spitting bullets he held in his mouth, directly down his gun barrel, he shot down four moose in a row. (Zaboly, *American Colonial Ranger*, 9)

For those with no basic knowledge of flintlock muzzle loading weapons, the lead ball, or bullet, is usually wrapped in a cloth patch or paper wadding before it is rammed down on top of the powder charge in the barrel of the musket or rifle. This gives a tight seal, which prevents the hot gases of the ignited powder charge from leaking around the ball as it exits the barrel, lessening the power of the shot. The patch or wadding also helps to stabilize the ball in the barrel. A typical lead ball is quite smaller in diameter than the inner diameter of the barrel, especially in a smoothbore musket. To spit an unpatched lead ball down a barrel, and still be accurate enough to kill four moose in a row, while loading as fast as possible, is truly an act of marksmanship.

The French also employed hunters, woodsmen, and native allies for their own scouting missions. These scouts were crack shots as well. These partisans also had the benefit of operating in their own territory. Their knowledge of the terrain and paths in the area would have been a definite advantage against the Ranger patrols. With this advantage, it would be easy to try to lure the Rangers into an ambush, where taking two men with one shot would be more likely. The loss of two men, whether killed or just wounded, would have seriously affected the ability of a small scouting party to withstand an attack, as well as the ability to go on the offensive against their enemy.

Rogers did not just expect his Rangers to follow this rule; he practiced it himself on many scouts against the French. Once, when on a scout near Ticonderoga and Crown Point, he and his Rangers ambushed some provision-laden sleys upon the frozen waters of Lake Champlain. Some of the enemy escaped and returned to Ticonderoga to spread the alarm that the Rangers were in the area:

> From this account of things, knowing that those who escaped would give early notice of us at Ticonderoga, I concluded it best to return; and ordered the party, with utmost expedition, to march to the fires we had kindled the night before. And prepare for a battle, it being a rainy, which we effected; and then marched in a single file, myself and Lieutenant Kennedy in the front, Lieutenant Stark in the rear and Captain Spikeman in the center. (Rogers, *Journals*, 37, 38)

The Rangers, especially early in the war, went on their scouting missions in relatively small groups, sometimes with as few as four or five men.

> Pursuant to orders of this date from Major-General Johnson, Commander in Chief of the Provincial Forces, raised for the reduction of Crown Point, I embarked with four men upon Lake George, to reconnoitre the strength of the enemy, and proceeding down the lake twenty five miles, I landed on the west side, leaving two men in charge of the boat. (Rogers, *Journals*, 1)

Not only did Rogers use a small party of five men on this scout, but also he left two men in charge of the boat, and then proceeded on his scout with only the other two remaining men.

The small size of the party would have minimized the amount of tracks they left behind, helping them to avoid detection. The encampment they were spying on at Crown Point held approximately five hundred men, but Rogers was still willing to risk the mission with just three men in his party, himself included.

Rogers also directed his Rangers to keep one or more men twenty yards out in front of the file as a forward guard to look for the approach of the enemy, and to guard against ambush. Additionally, he positioned one or more men at twenty yards to each side of the file to act as flankers, if the ground would permit it. Once again, Rogers wanted his men to be as prepared as possible to prevent being surprised. The advance man, or men, would be on the lookout for any sign or track of the enemy, while the flankers would be doing the same. If the advance guard missed an ambush by the enemy, by which the enemy would lay in concealment and let the Rangers pass until they could attack the whole of the party from either or both sides, the flanking parties were an additional safety measure against attack from the side. Even if the advanced guard missed the ambush, the enemy still had to hide from the flankers as well, increasing the chances of the Rangers discovering the enemy before they could spring their trap. The use of flanking parties by Rogers and the Rangers is well documented:

> A part of the Indian Company were sent out to the east side of Lake Champlain to alarm the enemy at Ticonderoga, whilst I, with a detachment of my own, and Capt. Richard Rogers company, was on another party ordered down Lake George in whale-boats, and the remainder of the companies were employed in reconnoitering round the encampment, and also served as flankers to the parties that guarded provisions to Lake George. (Rogers, *Journals*, 28)

The use of flanking parties depended that the ground in the area permitted this type of marching. Often the only paths were game trails, or those made by Indians. Rain, snow, ice, and mud would all hamper the ability of the Rangers to march in a single file in order to be prepared for the enemy.

By having an advanced guard in front of the file, the advanced man had a better chance to see the enemy approaching, so he could then inform the officer in charge as to the number in the enemy party, from what direction they were coming, how they were formed, and whether the Rangers had been seen. This would allow the Rangers to decide whether to attack, to try and hide and let the enemy pass them undetected, or to retreat in the face of superior numbers. If the Rangers decided to attack, the direction of the enemy would determine how they formed to their best advantage to meet the enemy.

At the "Second Battle on Snowshoes," Rogers' advanced guard gave him information of a column of Indians coming towards them on a frozen stream:

> In this manner we marched a mile and an half, when our advanced guard informed me of the enemy being in their view; and soon after, that they had ascertained their number to be ninety-six, chiefly Indians. (Rogers, *Journals*, 76)

By the advanced guard seeing the enemy first, and knowing the number of the enemy he was facing, Rogers was able to form his men to the best advantage for his ambush while remaining hidden from the enemy:

> We immediately laid down our packs, and prepared for battle, supposing these to be the whole number or main body of the enemy, who were marching on our left up the rivulet, upon the ice. I ordered Ensign McDonald to the command of the advanced guard, which we faced to the left and made a flanking party to our right. We marched to within a few yards of the bank, which was higher than the ground we ocupied; and observing the ground gradually to descend from the bank of the river to the foot of the mountain, we extended our party along the bank, far enough to command the whole of the enemy's at once; we waited till their front was nearly opposite to our left wing, when I fired a gun, as a signal for a general discharge upon them; whereupon we gave them the first fire, which killed above forty Indians. (Rogers, *Journals*, 76, 77)

Rogers would learn later that this party of "mostly Indians" was just the advanced guard of a much larger force. Rogers did make the most of this situation with the information he was given.

His men saw the enemy first, and were not detected. Using the numbers given, he thought he had sufficient numbers to attack. Rogers formed his line of battle, taking care to establish flanking parties on his right and left sides. He also chose the elevated bank of the river's edge to give his men the advantage of firing down at the enemy. This also made it harder for the enemy to counter attack, as they would have to scramble up the snow-covered, slippery bank of the stream in the face of the fire from the Rangers. The Rangers were also able to give the first fire to the enemy, in total surprise. This enabled the Rangers, marksmen that they were, to do substantial damage to the enemy's column. Although outnumbered, by following Rule Number Two, Rogers probably prevented the total annihilation of his command. Rogers and some of his men were able to escape under the cover of darkness and make their way back to Lake George, and then on to Fort Edward the next day.

Even though this battle turned into a major defeat for the Rangers, the importance and effectiveness of this method of marching is clear. Marching in a single file with the proper advanced guards and flankers kept the Rangers prepared to meet the enemy. Maintaining a proper distance between men prevented the killing of two men with one shot. These kinds of casualties could seriously undermine the chances of a successful mission. The Rangers had to be aware of their surroundings, even the ground upon which they marched. Small things like this could make the biggest difference. Once again, the emphasis of Rule Number Two is always to be prepared for any circumstance, so that reactions can be lightning-quick and the enemy can be attacked or repelled with vigor.

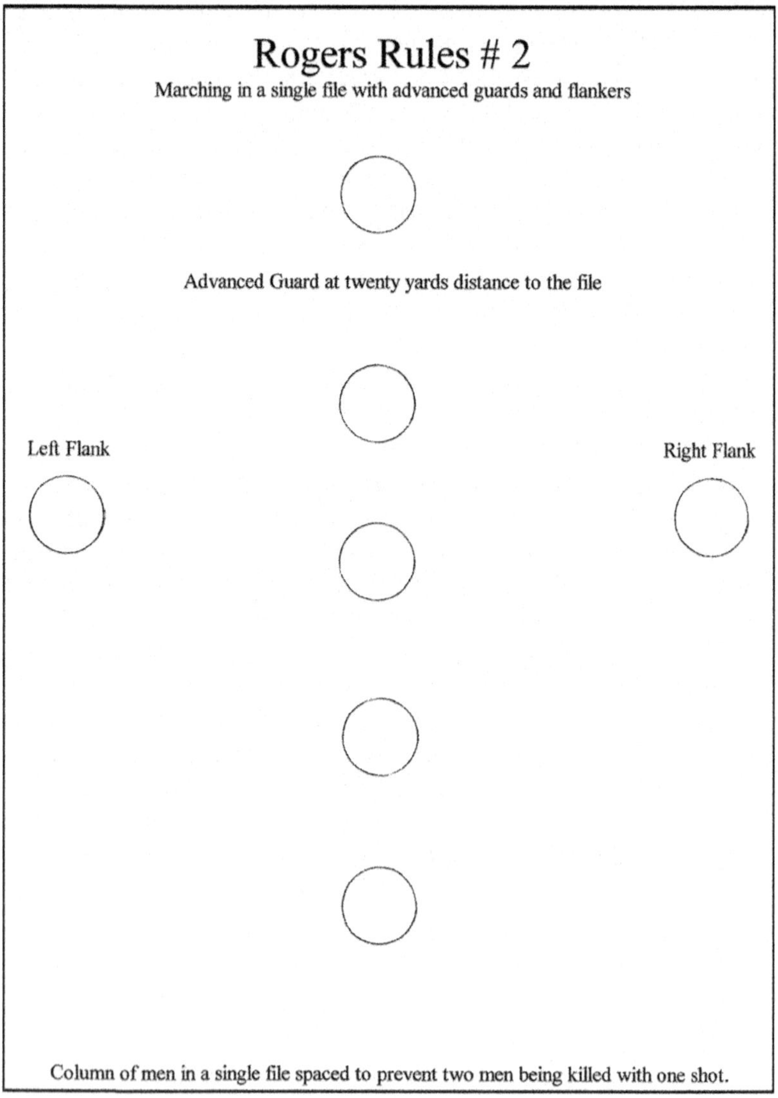

Rogers Rules # 2

Marching in a single file with advanced guards and flankers

Advanced Guard at twenty yards distance to the file

Left Flank

Right Flank

Column of men in a single file spaced to prevent two men being killed with one shot.

Figure 14.

Rogers' Rules: Number Three

If you march over marshes or soft ground, change your position, and march abreast of each other to prevent the enemy from tracking you (as they would do if you marched in a single file) till you get over such ground, and then resume your former order, and march till it is quite dark before you encamp, which do, if possible, on a piece of ground that may afford your centries the advantage of seeing or hearing the enemy some considerable distance, keeping one half of your whole party awake alternately through the night.

(Rogers, *Journals*, 72, 73)

The condition of the ground the Rangers marched upon determined how they marched, and in what type of formation. Marshes or soft ground presented problems for marching but Rule Number Three shows that Rogers could even turn a difficult situation to the Rangers' advantage.

An engraving by Thomas Johnston, printed in Boston in April 1756 shows a birds eye view of Fort William Henry and the retrenched camps on the west side of the fort. A huge area on this engraving between the fort and the retrenched camp is labeled as

"A Great Swamp." A copy of this engraving is shown on page 44 of Russell P. Bellico's book, *Sails and Steam in the Mountains: A Maritime and Military History of Lake George and Lake Champlain*. A manuscript map in John Cuneo's book, *Robert Rogers of the Rangers,* shows a large section of land to the southeast of Fort Ticonderoga labeled "Drowned Lands." (Cuneo illustration pages starting at 116) These two areas and countless others were the subjects of many of the Rangers' scouting missions. Ranger patrols from Fort William Henry and Fort Edward would have had to deal with these natural obstacles.

Rogers even used a swamp to a tactical advantage during a campaign to take the French strongholds at St. Jean and Chambly. While on this campaign, Rogers' landing of his men was discovered, and some of his Rangers spying on the French at Isle aux Noix warned him that three hundred native and French troops were pushing their way south to engage him:

> Rogers, forewarned, selected his terrain carefully, anchoring his right flank against a swamp. The French attacked his left flank as expected. Lieutenant Farrington with seventy men slipped around the bog along the lake shore to hit the French from the rear. When he opened his attack, Rogers 'pushed them in front.' Only a heavy downpour which allowed the enemy to scatter saved the French from annihilation. (Cuneo, 122)

One of the most difficult Ranger operations that involved traveling through a swamp was on the march to raid the Abenaki Indians at St. Francis. After embarking in whaleboats from Crown Point, the Rangers landed at Missisquoi Bay. It was here that the hardships of their journey began:

> Leaving their boats behind, the raiders now began a miserable nine-day march through the drowned lands, a seemingly endless swamp north of Missisquoi Bay. Marching through water a foot or more deep, the Rangers were forced to tie their moccasins to their feet to keep from losing them. At night, they would fashion platforms in the trees in which to sleep. (Todish, 86)

Mosquitoes and other insects were dreadful on this march. Many of the Rangers suffered from malaria and other illnesses years after this march because of the time spent in the swamps during the St. Francis raid, and countless others.

When crossing these areas of "soft ground," Rogers instructed his men to change from a single file formation to marching abreast. If the Rangers had marched in a single file on this type of ground, they would have left a very clear path, which would be easier for the French to discover. By spreading out, the amount of disturbance to the ground would be minimized, leaving less noticeable tracks for the French to find. Each man could pick his path carefully in order to avoid any great disruption to the ground. After the Rangers crossed this "soft ground or marshes," they were to resume their single file march for the reasons stated in Rule Number Two. Rogers did not specify having an advanced guard or flankers. We can assume that since the group was spread out to the sides, flankers were not be needed; but an advanced guard as well as the possible need for a rear guard was still likely. Rogers still would have needed to know of the approach of an enemy as soon as possible so he could form his men, especially in the difficult terrain of a swamp or "drowned lands."

When Rogers and his men attacked a group of woodcutters near Fort Carillon (Ticonderoga), they began their withdrawal by marching abreast, and when attacked, they merely faced about and met the enemy:

> And as we marched in a line abreast, our front was easily made. (Rogers, *Journals*, 119)

Rogers also wanted his men to march until dark before making their camp for the night. This minimized the chance of an enemy seeing them setting up a camp. If they made camp in the daylight, it would be easier for the French or their allies to see their position, and make the appropriate plans to attack the camp with this knowledge. By setting up camp in the darkness, the enemy had a difficult time knowing how the camp was set, and the disposition of the sentries.

> We landed this morning about fifteen miles down Lake George, and proceeded with the party till the 4th in the

evening, and encamped about a mile from the advanced guard. (Rogers, *Journals*, 22)

Rogers was confident enough traveling after dark that he was willing to make his camp within a mile of the enemy. He also kept his Rangers marching well into night, so that the darkness covered his movements and allowed him to get as close to his objective as possible:

> I went on my course till the 27th, towards Carillon, and landed that night on the west-side of the lake, concealed our boats, and traveled by land to within a mile of the fort. I kept spies out the day after to improve any opportunity that might offer, and the next day sent them still nearer, but to no good purpose. (Rogers, *Journals*, 31, 32)

Rogers encamped in that area during the next two days, trying to capture a prisoner or gain other intelligence of the enemy. The Rangers had to be very woods wise to be able to establish an encampment so near the enemy, while contending with what have could been a pitch black night.

The Rangers were also to establish their camp on a piece of ground higher in elevation than the surrounding area, which would enable them to see or hear the approach of the enemy. This rising ground would also give a good position from which to repel an attack. Rogers was known for using hills and the tops of mountains for his observations:

> I immediately sent an officer to wait upon the General for his orders, and received directions from Capt. Abercrombie, one of his Aide de Camps, to gain the top of a mountain that bore north about a mile from the landing-place, and from thence to steer east to the river that runs into the falls betwixt the landing and the saw-mill, to take possession of some rising ground on the enemy's side, and there to wait the army's coming. I immediately marched, ascended to the top of the hill, and from thence marched to the place I was ordered, where I arrived in about an hour, and posted my party to as good advantage as I could, being within one quarter of a mile of where Mons. Montcalm was posted with 1500 men, whom I had discovered by some small

reconnoitring parties sent out for that purpose. (Rogers, *Journals*, 102)

The possession of any rising ground in the area of the Rangers' operations was critical from a military standpoint, as well as the best place to set up camp to avoid detection by the enemy. The following reference gives further evidence of the importance of being posted on the "rising ground":

> I marched, agreeable to orders from the General, across the mountains in the isthmus; from thence, in a by-way, athwart the woods to the bridge at the Saw-mills; where finding the bridge standing, I immediately crossed it with my Rangers, and took possession of the rising ground on the other side, and beat from thence a party of the enemy, and took several prisoners, killed others, and put the remainder to flight, before Colonel Haviland with his grenadiers and light infantry got over. The army took possession that night of the heights near the Saw-mills, where they lay all evening. (Rogers, *Journals*, 126)

After the Rangers had taken possession of the best ground suited for their camp, which was often rising ground, they needed to be able to defend this ground from attack by the enemy. Rogers wanted proper sentries posted to warn of the enemy's approach. During the campaign against Ticonderoga and Crown Point in 1759, General Amherst received information from parties of Rangers constantly watching the enemy at Crown Point, that the French had blown up Fort St. Frederick and were retreating. He ordered Rogers to send a large party of Rangers to take possession of the fort.

> You are this night to send a Captain, with a proper proportion of subalterns, and two hundred men, to Crown Point, where the officer is to post himself in such a manner as not to be surprised, and to seize the best ground for defending himself; and if he should be attacked by the enemy, he is not to retreat with his party, but keep his ground till he is reinforced from the army. (Rogers, *Journals*, 129, 130)

Rogers also directed one-half of the men in a party to remain awake alternately through the night. With the campsite properly guarded with the necessary sentries, posted in the best positions possible, to warn of any trouble, and one half of the party awake at all times, the chance of being surprised is greatly reduced. Using the example of the party sent to Crown Point, over one hundred men would be awake and prepared to repel an enemy attack. The other half of the party that were sleeping, would be warned of the approach of the enemy by the sentries' alarm, and be prepared for the attack as well. It would be very hard to surprise such a well-guarded encampment.

We have learned from Rule Number Three that Rogers wanted his men to change their formation when marching over soft ground, and that he expected his men to march until darkness before making camp. The campsite was also to be on the most advantageous ground possible so the sentries could hear or see the approach of the enemy.

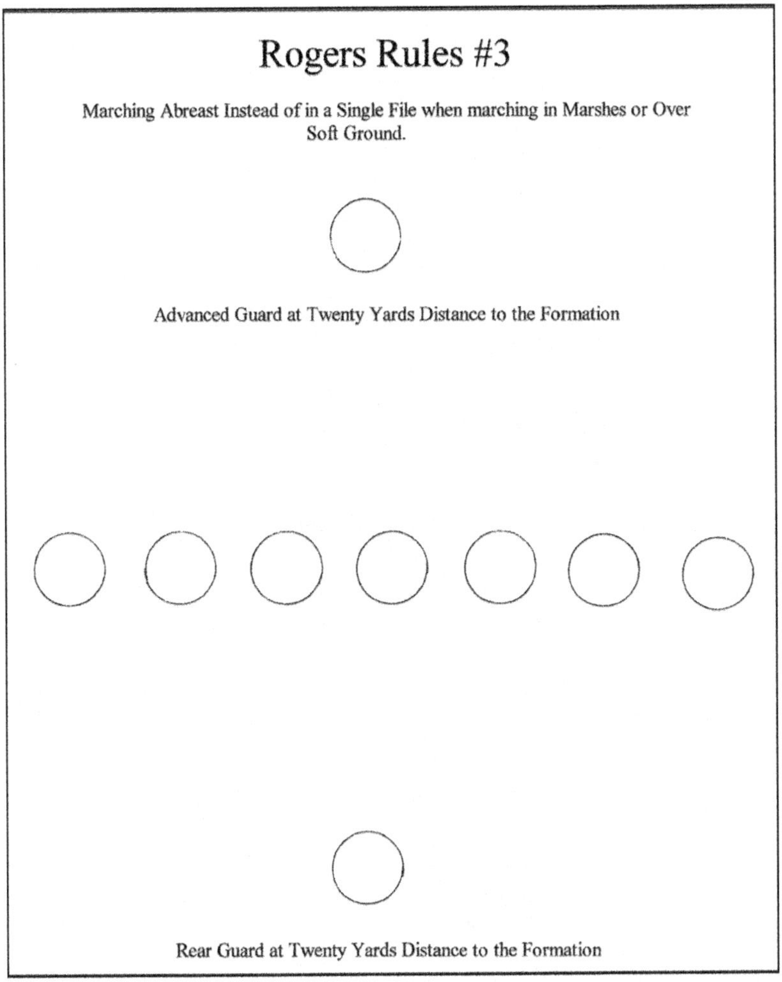

Rogers Rules #3

Marching Abreast Instead of in a Single File when marching in Marshes or Over Soft Ground.

Advanced Guard at Twenty Yards Distance to the Formation

Rear Guard at Twenty Yards Distance to the Formation

Figure 15.

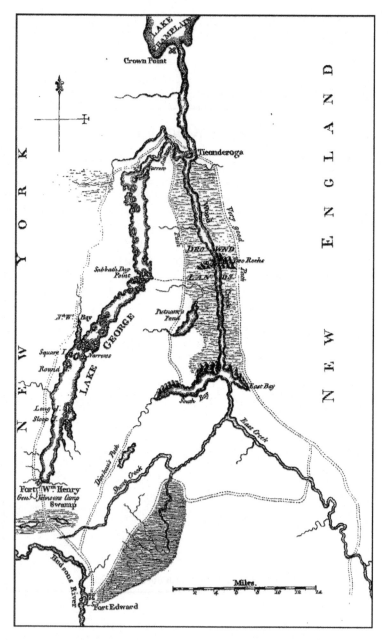

Figure 16. This period map of the Lake George–Lake Champlain corridor, from a copy in the author's collection, shows the swamps near Fort William Henry, and the large areas of "drowned lands" the Rangers had to march through on their scouts towards the French-held territories.

Rogers' Rules: Number Four

Some time before you come to the place you would reconnoitre, make a stand, and send one or two men in whom you can confide, to look out the best ground for making your observations.

(Rogers, *Journals*, 56)

After the Rangers reached their scouting destination, Rogers directed them to "make a stand" or prepare themselves for any circumstance that could occur in enemy territory.

Rogers and his Rangers were trying to gain intelligence of the numbers of troops stationed at the French forts as well as any plans or operations against the British Army. One of the best ways to accomplish this was to take prisoners who could reveal vital information. Thus, the Rangers had to penetrate deep into French occupied territory, which meant slipping past the French troops, their Native American allies, and the local inhabitants. The locals, even though they may not have been combatants, would surely raise the alarm of the Rangers being in the area. By first making a defensive stand, the scouts would be able to resist an attack in the event of discovery by the enemy. In order to take advantage of any intelligence gained by their scouts, the Rangers would first have to return safely to their base of operations.

October 21, 1755. I had orders from General Johnson of this
date, to embark for Crown Point, with a party of four men in
quest of a prisoner. At night we landed on the west-side of
Lake George, twenty-five miles from the English camp. The
remainder of the way we marched by land, and the 26th
came in sight of the fort. In the evening we approached
nearer, and the next day found ourselves within about 300
yards of it. My men lay concealed in a thicket of willows,
while I crept something nearer, to a large pine log, where I
concealed myself, by holding bushes in my hand. (Rogers,
Journals, 5)

Rogers often went ahead by himself, or sent others forward to
reconnoiter their destination after the remainder of the party had
"made their stand." The small forward party could observe the
enemy inconspicuously and from a smaller piece of ground than
would be required for the entire party, lessening the likelihood of
discovery. Rogers used this tactic when scouting the Abenaki
Indian village at St. Francis:

The twenty-second day after my departure from Crown
Point, I came in sight of the Indian town St. Francis in the
evening, which I discovered from a tree I had climbed, at
about three miles distance. Here I halted my party, which
now consisted of 142 men, officers included, being reduced
to that number by the unhappy accident which befel Capt.
Williams, and several since tiring, whom I was obliged to
send back. At eight o'clock this evening I left the
detachment, and took with me Lieut. Turner and Ensign
Avery, and went to reconnoitre the town, which I did to my
satisfaction, and found the Indians in a high frolic or dance.
I returned to my party at two o'clock, and at three marched
it to within five hundred yards of the town, where I
lightened the men of their packs, and formed them for the
attack. (Rogers, *Journals*, 133, 134)

While Rogers, Turner, and Avery scouted the Abenaki village,
the rest of the Rangers waited in darkness, having made their
stand. They already knew that the French had discovered their
boats and were hot on the Rangers' trail. Word would soon spread

that the Rangers were in the area, and the whole country would be on the lookout for them. Constant vigilance was imperative.

Rogers also was not above sending out men "in whom you can confide" to scout or spy on the enemy, once the rest of the men had made their stand. These men risked not only their own lives, but possibly the lives of the whole party, if they were discovered.

Rule Number Four is well illustrated in this description of a scout for General William Johnson on November 4, 1755:

> The next morning, a little before day-light, we arrived within half a mile of them, where we landed, and concealed our boats; I then sent out four men as spies, who returned the next evening, and informed me, that the enemy had no works round them, but lay entirely open to an assault; which advice I dispatched immediately to the General, desiring a sufficient force to attack them, which, notwithstanding the General's earnestness and activity in the affair, did not arrive until we were obliged to retreat. On our return, however, we were met by reinforcement, sent by the General, whereupon I returned again towards the enemy, and the next evening sent two men to see if the enemy's centries were alert, who approached so near as to be discovered and fired at by them, and were so closely pursued in their retreat, that unhappily our whole party was discovered. (Rogers, *Journals*, 5, 6)

The final requirement of Rule Number Four, "the best ground for your observations," would have been elevated ground if at all possible, for the same reasons stated in Rule Number Three:

> A popular gathering spot that gave an excellent view of Fort Ticonderoga was Rattlesnake Mountain, or as it was later known, Mount Defiance. From this vantage point, the Rangers were treated to an almost full-view of Ticonderoga…including the comings and goings of troops, native allies, and French shipping along Lake Champlain. (Matheney, 9)

From these elevated points, the Rangers would make their observations through telescopes or "perspective glasses":

We halted at a place called Sabbath-Day Point, on the west -
side of the lake, and sent our parties to look down the lake
with perspective glasses, which we had for that purpose.
(Rogers, *Journals*, 74)

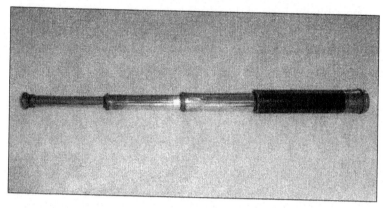

Figure 17. A reproduction brass telescope or "perspective glass" of the
style that was used by the Rangers in the eighteenth century. It is a four-
section model, which collapses to take up less room in the pack or
haversack.

Rogers and his Rangers spied on the French from high points
on the hills and mountains that surround Lake George and Lake
Champlain. Telescopes like the one shown allowed them to make
observations from a greater distance, in greater safety.
A diagram drawn by Rogers illustrates the amount of vital
information, as to the defenses of the enemy, the Rangers provided
to the British war effort. On one of his first scouts in support of Sir
William Johnson after the "Battle of Lake George," Rogers drew a
plan of the French fort known as St. Frederick, at Crown Point. He
made his observations from an elevated position, or "eminence,"
to the southwest of the fort, possibly on a small rocky ledge now
known as "Coot Hill." Rogers' drawing shows the outline of the
the fort, the outbuildings, and an external battery that the French
forces were building.

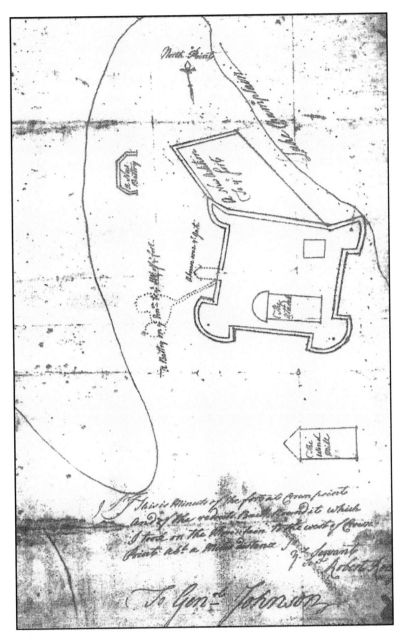

Figure 18. A copy of an original drawing that Robert Rogers drew on one of his first scouts in support of Sir William Johnson after the "Battle of Lake George." Courtesy of the Crown Point Historical Site and the Library of Congress.

Rogers' Rule Number Four points out the effectiveness of using a telescope in combination with the natural advantage of an elevated observation position to gain a tactical advantage. Information gained from these scouts into French-held territory was vital. A small group of Rangers, operating in advance of a larger group, had a greater chance of passing through the enemy lines and gathering the desired intelligence without discovery.

Rogers' Rules: Number Five

If you have the Good fortune to take any prisoners, keep them separate, till they are examined, and in your return take a different route from that in which you went out, that you may better discover any party in your rear, and have an opportunity, if their strength be superior to yours, to alter your course, or disperse, as circumstances may require.

(Rogers, *Journals*, 56)

As we have already learned, Rogers was often ordered to try to capture prisoners because of the valuable information they could provide:

> I kept spies out the day after to improve any opportunity that might offer, and the next day sent them still nearer, but to no good purpose: I at length discovered two men centries to the piquet guard of the French army, one of which was posted on the road that leads from the fort to the woods: I took five of my party, and marched directly down the road in the middle of the day, till we were challenged by the centry. I answered in French, signifying that we were friends; the centinel was thereby deceived, till I came close to him, when perceiving his mistake, in great surprise he

called Qui etes vous? I answered Rogers, and led him from his post in great haste, cutting his breeches and coat from him, that he might march with the greater ease and expedition. With this prisoner we arrived at Fort William-Henry, Oct. 31, 1756. Upon examination, he reported, "That he belonged to the regiment of Lanquedoc: that he left Brest last April was a twelve-month, and had served since at Lake Champlain, Crown Point, and Carillon, was last year with General Dieskaw in the battle at Fort William-Henry: that they lost in that engagement of regulars, Canadians, and Indians, a great number: and at Carillon were at this time mounted thirty six pieces of cannon, viz. twelve eighteen pounders, fifteen twelve pounders, and nine eight pounders, that at Crown Point were eighteen pieces, the largest of which were eighteen pounders: that Mons. Montcalm's forces this year at Carillon were 3000 regulars, and 2000 Canadians and Indians. (Todish/Zaboly, 55)

This particular prisoner revealed a great amount of vital information. Most captives were highly reluctant to give up any details that would undermine French interests. Rogers stressed that the prisoners be kept separate until they could be questioned, so that they could not concoct a story between them by which to deceive the Rangers and the British command. The Rangers could not afford to plan a scout or an attack based on false reports from prisoners.

We pursued them, and took seven prisoners, three sleds, and six horses; the remainder made their escape. We examined the captives separately, who reported, that 200 Canadians and 45 Indians were just arrived at Ticonderoga, and were to be reinforced that evening, or next morning, by fifty Indians more from Crown Point; that there were 600 regular troops at that fortress, and 350 at Ticonderoga, where they soon expected a large number of troops, who in the spring were to besiege our forts, and that they had large magazines of provisions in their forts, and that the above mentioned party were well equipped, and in a condition to march upon any emergency at the least notice, and were designed soon to way-lay and distress our convoys between our forts. (Rogers, *Journals*, 32, 33)

By examining the captives separately, the Rangers could compare their stories, and determine if the information given to them was correct. Had they been examined together, some of the prisoners might have been reluctant to speak in the presence of their friends or superior officers. In one case a French deserter was questioned in the presence of a captured French officer after the successful siege of Quebec:

A deserter from one of the enemy's advanced posts, informs us that the French troops are so inconceivably distressed, for all kinds of provisions, and liquors, that their perseverance is astonishing; he adds that their numbers may amount to twelve thousand, including savages, etc. who are all so dispersed and at their liberty to shift for themselves that they scarcely deserve the name of an army. When this fellow was brought before the governor, there was a French officer present who is on his parole: he seemed disconcerted at the admission of the deserter, and swaggered about the apartment in great wrath. (Knox, *Siege of Quebec*, 237)

Rogers advised his men in returning from a scout to "take a different route from that in which you went out." This way the men were able to watch their back trail and see if the enemy, who may have discovered their tracks, was pursuing them. If the Rangers' trail was discovered, the French could lay an ambush on that trail, waiting for the to Rangers return along the same route.

Rogers himself was guilty of breaking this rule once with dire consequences. After capturing the sleys and prisoners between Crown Point and Ticonderoga as mentioned earlier, the French troops who escaped certainly would have spread the alarm. The French and Indians stationed at Ticonderoga were well-equipped and ready to travel. The Rangers were in desperate danger of being cut off from their retreat back to Fort William Henry.

I concluded it best to return; and ordered the party, with the utmost expedition, to march to the fires we had kindled the night before, and prepare for a battle, if it should be offered, by drying our guns, it being a rainy day, which we effected; and then marched in a single file. (Rogers, *Journals*, 37)

Rogers had his reasons for breaking his own rule, however. The Rangers' guns were soaked by the rain, and the firewood in the area was wet, so he felt it best to march back to the camp of the night before, where some coals might remain, making it easier to start fires and dry out their muskets. Without working firelocks, the coming battle might have turned into total annihilation of the Ranger party. Rogers also may have hoped that he and his party had reacted quickly enough to get past the French before they had a chance to set their trap. Unfortunately, this was not the case:

In this manner we advanced half a mile, or thereabouts, over broken ground, when passing a valley of about fifteen rods breadth, the front having reached the summit of a hill on the west-side of it; the enemy, who were drawn up in the form of a half-moon, with a design, as we supposed, to surround us, saluted us with a volley of about 200 shot, at the distance of about five yards from the nearest or front, and thirty from the rear of their party. This fire was about 2 o'clock in the afternoon, and proved fatal to Lieutenant Kennedy and Mr. Gardner, a volunteer in my company, and wounded me and several others; myself, however, but slightly in the head. (Rogers, *Journals*, 38)

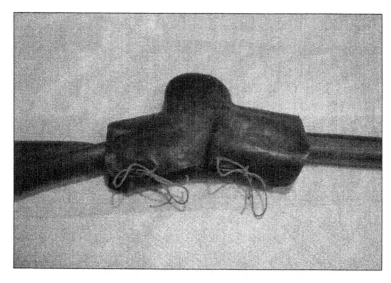

Figure 19. A greased leather cover, or "cow's knee," which wraps around the lock area of the musket to keep the lock, flint, and priming charge from getting wet. If the priming charge becomes wet, it renders the musket useless except as a club. The Rangers used these simple covers to try to "waterproof" their firelocks during rain, snow, or other wet conditions.

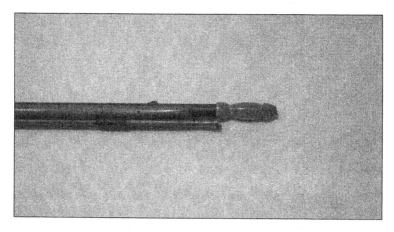

Figure 20. A turned wooden barrel plug, or "tompion," protected the main powder charge by sealing the end of the musket barrel. These plugs were easily removed to fire the weapon. This was another item the Rangers used to prevent wet weather from fouling the powder charge in their muskets while on the march, or on other duty.

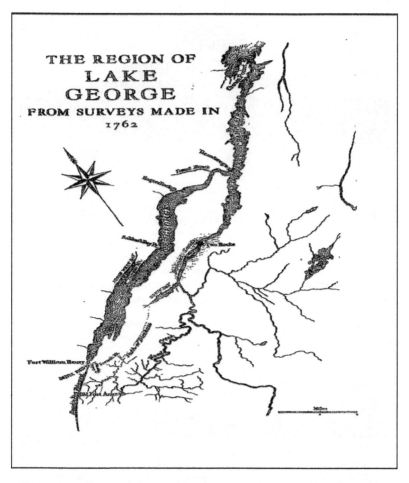

Figure 21. This map, from a copy in the author's collection, shows the Lake George–Lake Champlain corridor as it looked during the French and Indian War. This was the main area of operations for the Rangers under Robert Rogers' command during this conflict.

Rogers' Rules:
Number Six

If you march in a large body of three or four hundred, with a design to attack the enemy, divide your party into three columns, each headed by a proper officer, and let these columns march in single files, the columns to the right and left keeping at twenty yards distance or more from the center, if the ground will admit, and let proper guards be directed, with orders to halt on all eminences, to take a view of the surrounding ground, to prevent your being ambuscaded, and to notify the approach or retreat of the enemy, that proper dispositions may be made for attacking, defending &c. And if the enemy approach in your front on level ground, form a front of your three columns or main body with the advanced guard, keeping out your flanking parties, as if you were marching under the command of trusty officers, to prevent the enemy from pressing hard on either of your wings, or surrounding you, which is the usual method of the savages, if their numbers will admit of it, and be careful likewise to support and strengthen your rear-guard.

(Rogers, *Journals*, 56)

Rogers' Rule Number Six describes the formation he thought best suited for marching with a large body of men. In the beginning of the French and Indian War, the Rangers normally conducted their scouts in small numbers, but as the war progressed, these formations expanded to several hundred men, including at times Regular troops and elements of the Light Infantry. The British advanced up the Ticonderoga peninsula in this type of formation prior to the Battle of Carillon in 1758. General Montcalm described the advancing British formation:

> About one o'clock our detachments, and grenadiers, who were in advance, perceived the enemy approaching in three columns, they all came in without any confusion. The signal was given, and the following instant the three columns were seen defiling; the 1st towards the left of the intrenchment, the 2nd against the center; the 3rd, which appeared the strongest, marching towards the bottom, on the right of the hill. Some Indians and Rangers went in front as guides. (Todish/Zaboly 128)

This style of formation allowed easy adjustment of columns to meet the enemy. When the enemy was sighted, the three columns formed into ranks in combination with the advanced guard. The flanking parties took their positions on the right and left, and the rear guard maintained its position protecting the rear. The size of the area determined how the main force was deployed onto the front, how many ranks, etc. If the area was small, the deployment may have been changed to small squads or some other method of firing positions.

During the 1758 campaign against Carillon (Ticonderoga), Rogers, with about two hundred Rangers, secured the rising ground near the French sawmills. A Provincial force under the command of Colonels Lyman and Fitch soon joined them there. As the colonels and Rogers held a council, a fight broke out in the rear of the Provincials' column:

> While this conversation passed, a sharp fire began in the rear of Col. Lyman's regiment, on which he said he would make his front immediately, and desiring me to fall on their left flank, which I accordingly did, having first ordered

Capt. Burbanks with 150 men to remain at the place I was posted, to observe the motions of the French at the saw-mills, and went with the remainder of the Rangers on the left flank of the enemy, the river being on their right, and killed several. (Rogers, *Journals*, 102, 103)

Great care was taken here to protect the flanks, with Rogers covering the left side, and the river covering the right. Rogers also took the initiative to leave a force of one hundred and fifty men in his rear to watch the enemy in that direction. This rear guard would prevent an attack from the rear, and could have been used as a reserve force to strengthen other areas as well.

There are many ways to go from files to ranks, but speed in reforming is critical in order to present a formidable front to the enemy, whether to attack or to insure an adequate defense.

The direction of the attack from the opposing force will determine how to form the men. If approached from either the right or the left flank, that flank then becomes the advanced guard, forming the front with the main body. The advanced guard becomes the right or left flank depending on the direction of attack. If attacked or opposed from the rear, the rear guard becomes the advanced guard, and the advanced guard becomes the rear guard. The flanking parties maintain their positions on the flanks by a right and left about to face the enemy. If the attack comes from the flanks, it would be very easy to face to the right or left to form ranks to the direction of opposition. Again, speed is essential in these movements in order to form the front to attack, or to defend against an attack. Some of the ranks may be held in reserve to strengthen the flanks or the rear guard if necessary. They may also be used to strengthen the front in order to push the enemy, or if the enemy tries to push the front.

Rogers used these methods when his Rangers were marching with Lieutenant Colonel Bradstreet's batteaumen and Gage's Light Infantry in the previously discussed advance against Ticonderoga in 1758:

I was within about three hundred yards of the breast-work, when my advanced guard was ambushed and fired upon by about 200 Frenchmen. I immediately formed a front, and marched up to the advanced guard, who maintained their ground, and the enemy immediately retreated; soon after the battoe-men formed on my left and light infantry on my right. (Rogers, *Journals*, 103, 104)

As put forth in Rule Number Six, Rogers used the advanced guard in combination with his columns to form a front, which repulsed the enemy (see Figure 23). Rogers also was careful in his use of the men held in reserve, in case the enemy was able to push the center, or one of the flanks. Rogers made good use of these reserves to beat back the attacks of the French in the "First Battle on Snowshoes" in January of 1757:

I then ordered my men to the opposite hill, where I supposed Lieutenant Stark and Ensign Brewer had made a stand with forty men to cover us, in case we were obliged to retreat. We were closely pursued, and Capt. Spikeman, with several of the party, were killed, and others made prisoners. My people, however beat them back by a brisk fire from the hill, which gave us an opportunity to ascend, and post ourselves to advantage. After which I ordered Lieutenant Stark and Mr. Baker in the center, with Ensign Rogers; Sergeants Walter and Phillips, with a party, being a reserve, to prevent our being flanked, and watch the motions of the enemy. Soon after we had thus formed ourselves for battle, the enemy attempted to flank us on the right, but the above reserve bravely attacked them, and giving them the first fire very briskly, it stopped several from retreating to the main body. (Rogers, *Journals*, 38, 39)

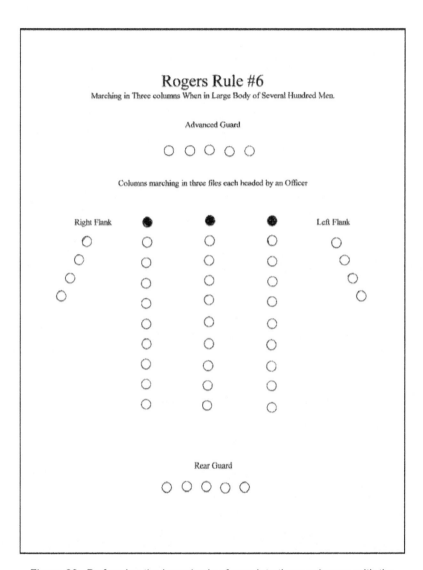

Figure 22. By forming the large body of men into three columns, with the proper advanced and rear guards and flankers, the party could be quickly formed to meet any enemy attack, with reserves being maintained to prevent the sections from being overwhelmed.

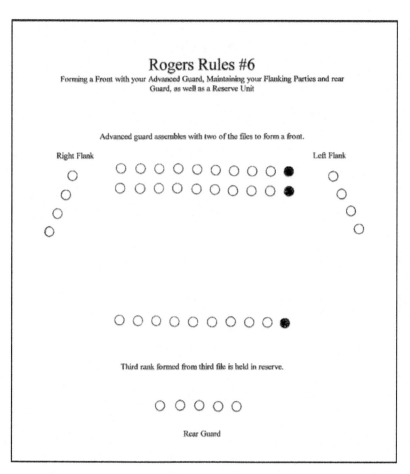

Rogers Rules #6

Forming a Front with your Advanced Guard, Maintaining your Flanking Parties and rear Guard, as well as a Reserve Unit

Advanced guard assembles with two of the files to form a front.

Right Flank   Left Flank

Third rank formed from third file is held in reserve.

Rear Guard

Figure 23. As stated in Rule Number Six, Rogers used the advanced guard in combination with his columns to form a front, which repulsed the enemy.

Rogers' Rules: Number Seven

If you are obliged to receive the enemy's fire, fall, or squat down, till it is over, then rise and discharge at them. If their main body is equal to yours, extend yourself occasionally; but if superior, be careful to support and strengthen your flanking parties, to make them equal to theirs, that if possible you may repulse them to their main body, in which case push upon them with the greatest resolution with equal force in each flank and in the center, observing to keep at a due distance from each other ten or twelve yards. If the enemy push upon you, let your front fire and fall down, and then let your rear advance thro' them and do the like, by which time those who before were in front will be ready to discharge again, and repeat the same alternately, as occasion shall require; by this means you will keep up such a constant fire, that the enemy will not be able easily to break your order, or gain your ground.

(Rogers, *Journals*, 57, 58)

Rogers and his Rangers found themselves ambushed by French forces several times during the course of the French and Indian War, two of them being the "First Battle on Snowshoes," and the "Battle at Fort Anne." The French threw a murderous volley into the Ranger scout at the Battle on Snowshoes:

> A crescent-shaped fusilade brought down several of the leading Rangers as the men reached the crest of the far side of the ravine. Rogers himself received a glancing head wound. Covered by volleys from the rest of his party in position on the opposite ridge, Rogers led his survivors back across the stream and there organized a stand. (Todish, 41)

Rogers formed his men accordingly, using the rising ground of the ridge to make his stand, keeping out flanking parties, and forming a reserve under Sergeants Walter and Phillips. The Rangers then began to give the enemy a brisk fire, which repulsed them back to their main body of troops, leaving several men behind dead. By pushing this attack back in to their main body, the enemy troops became confused and in disarray, with the wounded and retreating men being mixed in with the main body. This would have been a perfect time for Rogers and his force to push them in the center and on the flanks due to their confusion, but being outnumbered, and having lost a large number of his men at the outset of the ambush, they were not able to attempt this. Due to superior numbers of the enemy, Rogers on several occasions was not able to pursue an advantage gained by the constant fire of his Rangers:

> The remainder I rallied, and drew up in pretty good order, where they fought with such intrepidity and bravery as obliged the enemy (tho' seven to one in number) to retreat a second time; but not being in a condition to pursue them, they rallied again, and recovered their ground, and warmly pushed us in front and both wings; while the mountain defended our rear; but they were warmly received, that their flanking parties soon retreated to their main body with considerable loss. This threw the whole again into disorder, and they retreated a third time. (Rogers, *Journals*, 77, 78)

Here Rogers strictly adhered to the tenets of Rule Number Seven, strengthening his flanks and center when pushed upon by a superior force. The enemy was constantly driven back to their main force under much confusion, but had Rogers tried to push his men forward, the French, having numbers far superior to that of the Rangers, probably would have flanked Rogers' force and totally defeated them. If Rogers had pushed the French at that point he would have given up his advantage of the strong defensive position of the ridge, with the mountain at his rear, which greatly aided his outnumbered force in resisting the French attacks. Rogers and his Rangers had to be very cautious about knowing when and when not to try to push the enemy.

When pursuing Bougainville's retreating forces from Isle a Mott, Rogers fell onto the French rear guard of 200 men, and attacked them with a party of 400 men and two companies of Indians. Even though the main French force consisted of 1500 troops and 100 Indians, Rogers and his party forced the French to retreat across a river, where they pulled up the bridge and escaped.

> I got so well fortified, that I ventured our boats and baggage under the care of 200 Rangers, and took with me 400, together with two companies of Indians, and followed after the French army, which consisted of about 1500 men, and about 100 Indians, they had to guard them. I was resolved to make his dance a little merrier, and pursued with such haste, that I overtook his rear guard about two miles before they got to their encamping ground. I immediately attacked them, who not being above 200, suddenly broke, and then stood for the main body, which I very eagerly pursued, but in good order, expecting Monsieur Bonville would have made a stand, which however he did not chuse, but pushed forward to get to the river, where they were to encamp, and having crossed it, pulled up the bridge, which put a stop to my march. (Rogers, *Journals*, 175, 176)

Rogers again illustrated the importance of keeping a proper distance between his men. Men bunched together made a larger target for the French and Indian marksmen. The French were also known for firing a combination of a ball and buckshot in their weapons, just as the Rangers sometimes did. Another unique and

deadly load was employed by the French during the siege of
Quebec:

> Some buccaneer firelocks, of an uncommon length, were
> found by our men to-day, buried in an orchard adjoining to
> the great watermill; upon examining them, they were loaded
> with two balls each, besides a piece of square iron, four
> inches long, the edges of which were wickedly filed rough,
> like the teeth of a saw. (Knox, *Siege of Quebec*, 139)

We cannot be sure of the style of these firelocks, but they were
not swivel guns, as this term would have been used to describe
them. They might have been heavy, large caliber wall guns.
Rogers himself had used what he called "wall-pieces" mounted on
some bateaus in a scout up Lake George in 1755.

Keeping a constant fire in the face of the enemy was vital to
the often-outnumbered Rangers. We have already learned that the
majority of the Rangers, most of them being skilled frontier
hunters, were excellent marksmen:

> There are no better marksmen in the world, for their whole
> delight is shooting at marks for wages. (Zaboly, *American
> Colonial Ranger*, 14)

The Rangers, unlike the Regulars, would use any cover
available to minimize themselves as targets. Instead of volley fire,
where all of the troops would discharge their weapons at once, the
Rangers fired only when a fellow soldier had reloaded his firelock,
and could then cover the partner in his "fire team." This would
prevent the French and their native allies from rushing upon the
Rangers when all of their guns were empty.

> Tactics employed by Captain James Smith on the
> Pennsylvania frontier during Pontiac's War were largely
> familiar to Rogers. For instance, Smith would assign every
> two of his rangers "to take a tree"... with orders to keep a
> reserve fire, one not to fire until his comrade had loaded his
> gun – by this means we kept up a constant, slow fire.

Once a captive of the Indians, Smith wrote a treatise on their
manner of fighting and asked the questions:

Why have we not made greater proficiency in the Indian art of war? Is it because we are too proud to imitate them, even though it should be a means of preserving the lives of many of our citizens? (Zaboly, *American Colonial Ranger*, 21)

The Rangers often practiced their methods of bush fighting and engaging and firing at the enemy. The journal of Connecticut Provincial soldier Abel Spicer attests to the seriousness that Rogers placed on being able to maintain this type of firing against the enemy, by practicing these maneuvers and firings.

This day in the afternoon Major Rogers took his men without the camp beyond the advance guard to exercise them in the woods to skulk and to fire as to engage the enemy. The General went to see them and several of the chief officers. (Todish/Zaboly, 79)

Rogers' men practiced the method of holding one rank or fire team member in reserve, while the first rank discharged their pieces at the enemy. The second rank would then advance through the first and push against the enemy. By the time the second rank was in position, and had discharged their firelocks, the first rank would have then been reloaded, and would be able to advance through the second rank, thereby advancing against the enemy while maintaining a constant fire against them. The rank that had discharged their weapons would fall, or squat down to minimize the size of the target they made, as the other rank passed by them. They could even reload from their bellies, or in a squatting position. Many of the New England troops were able to load in this manner.

The New England troops, according to an eyewitness in Nova Scotia, could "load their firelocks upon their back, then turn upon their bellies, and take aim at their enemies." (Zaboly, *American Colonial Ranger*, 14)

Rogers and his men employed this tactic when the British army assaulted the French outer defensive lines during the 1758 campaign against Fort Ticonderoga. The Rangers were ordered to engage the enemy that was stationed outside of these works. A skirmish ensued, where a brisk fire from the Rangers forced the

French back behind their lines. The Rangers then fell down, and let the Regulars march through them and assault the works.

About half an hour past ten, the greatest part of the enemy being drawn up, a smart fire began on our left wing, where col. DeLancey's, (the New Yorkers,) and the battoe-men were posted, upon which I was ordered forward to endeavor to beat the enemy within the breast-work, and then fall down, that the pickets and grenadiers might march through. (Rogers, *Journals*, 104)

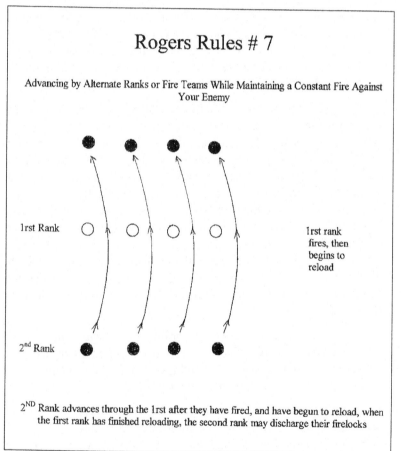

Figure 24. Advancing by alternate ranks while maintaining a constant fire.

Rogers Rules # 7

Advancing by Alternate Ranks or Fire Teams While Maintaining a Constant Fire Against Your Enemy

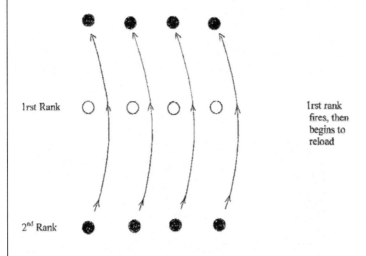

1rst Rank

1rst rank fires, then begins to reload

2nd Rank

2ND Rank advances through the 1rst after they have fired, and have begun to reload, when the first rank has finished reloading, the second rank may discharge their firelocks

Figure 24.

Figure 26.

Figure 27. This photo shows the methods Robert Rogers taught his Rangers to use when advancing against their enemy. The Ranger in front is holding his position, and reserving his fire, while a Ranger Officer orders the second Ranger to advance. By doing this, the first Ranger covers the movements of the advancing Ranger. If the second Ranger fires his musket at the enemy, the first Ranger will still have a loaded weapon. After the advancing Ranger has reloaded, the second Ranger may hold his ground and fire, or advance and fire as the Ranger before him did. This allows a constant fire against the enemy, while advancing and putting pressure on the enemy's front, possibly causing them to break.

Rogers and his men of course, used any cover available to protect themselves, but the Regulars marched in the open against the French works time and time again, with disastrous results. The French troops fired volley after volley into the advancing British troops, decimating their ranks, until General Abercromby ordered a halt to the operations and ordered a full retreat back to their camp at the south end of Lake George. Any assault on Fort Ticonderoga was finished for the year, except for scouting missions by the Rangers in the direction of Carillon.

Rogers' Rules: Number Eight

If you oblige the enemy to retreat, be careful, in your pursuit of them, to keep out your flanking parties, and prevent them from gaining eminences, or rising grounds, in which case they would perhaps be able to rally and repulse you in their turn.

(Rogers, *Journals*, 58)

At the "Battle of Bernetz Riviere" or what is also known as the "Second Battle on Snowshoes," Rogers and his Rangers ambushed what they thought was a party of ninety-six men, most of them Indians, marching along the frozen surface of a river. This party actually turned out to be the advanced guard of a much larger force of French troops. After the initial volley, in which Rogers estimated the Rangers killed about forty of the enemy, he ordered his advanced guard to pursue them, while he and the remainder of his party stayed behind and scalped the dead. Rogers' advanced guard, under the command of Ensign Gregory McDonald, their blood up, charged after the fleeing French and Indians:

> I now imagined the enemy totally defeated, and ordered Ensign M'Donald to head the flying remains of them, that none might escape; but we soon found our mistake, and that the party we had attacked were only their advanced guard,

their main body coming up, consisting of 600 more, Canadians and Indians; upon which I ordered our people to retreat to their own ground, which we gained at the expense of fifty men killed. (Rogers, *Journals*, 77)

When Rogers ordered his men to pursue the fleeing remnants of the enemy's advanced guard, he split his party in half, which severely weakened the force sent out to pursue the enemy. Rogers did not state what type of formation they were in, but we can assume that they were literally chasing after the enemy like a pack of dogs going in for the kill. When they were met and fired upon by the main body of the French force, the Rangers were caught off guard and had to flee for their lives back to their original position. Had the Rangers formed themselves with advanced guards and flanking parties, they may have discovered their mistake earlier and prevented some of the fifty deaths they incurred. The Rangers were able to retreat and rally, finally pushing the enemy back and forcing them to retreat. The loss of so many men, combined with the fact that the Rangers were outnumbered, turned this occasion into one of their greatest defeats.

That Rogers was able to gain some rising ground and rally his troops shows how a retreating force can use the ground to its advantage. At the "Battle of Fort Anne," the Rangers were able to force the French to retreat, but were unable to press them because of the orderly French withdrawal. Mante gives this account:

Both he (Rogers) and his men behaved with such spirit, that, in an hour, they broke the assailants, and obliged them to retreat, though (such was the enemy's caution) without any prospect of being able to distress them by a pursuit. (Todish/Zaboly, 144)

Even in retreat, the French forces withdrew with good order, making a pursuit by the Rangers a risky undertaking. The French probably had deployed a substantial rear guard as well as flanking parties as they marched away from the field of battle. The use of flanking parties has been well documented and stressed in the previous rules we have discussed. European linear tactics, which used massed frontal assaults against the enemy's formations or defensive works, also made use of flanking maneuvers in different tactical situations. In the woodlands and swamps of colonial

America, the use of flanking parties was critical, even in a strong defensive position. During the Battle of Fort Anne, some French troops had taken up a position behind the trunk of a fallen tree. The Regulars and Light Infantry advanced against this opposition.

> A party of French & Indians who had taken post behind a tree that had fallen down; the Regulars and Light Infantry Advanc'd and Flank'd the Tree; beat them off and took possession of the Contrary side. (Todish/Zaboly, 146)

Either the French had not deployed flanking parties, or they were not strong enough to resist the British attack on their flanks, for they were forced to retreat. Some French reinforcements made a counterattack, and a fierce battle raged until Major Rogers entered the scene with some additional troops and forced the French to retreat for good, leaving behind about 100 of their dead.

The Native Americans were well known for their tactic of sweeping around the flanks of the enemy and eventually surrounding them. The Reverend William Smith, in his historical account of the Expedition of Colonel Henry Bouquet against the Ohio Indians in 1764, discusses this tactic:

> Let us suppose a person, who is entirely unacquainted with the nature of this service, to be put at the head of an expedition in America. We will further suppose that he has made the dispositions usual in Europe for a march, or to receive an enemy; and that he is then attacked by the savages. He cannot discover them, tho' from every tree, log or bush, he receives an incessant fire, and observes that few of their shot are lost. He will not hesitate to charge those invisible enemies, but he will charge in vain. For they are as cautious to avoid a close engagement, as indefatigable in harassing his troops; and notwithstanding all his endeavors, he will still find himself surrounded by a circle of fire, which like a artificial horizon follows him every where. (Todish/Zaboly, 258)

This method of encircling the enemy after sweeping down his sides was what doomed the expedition under General Braddock against the French at Fort Duquesne in 1755. Many people over the years have said that Braddock's force fell into an enemy ambush, and that his march was not prepared for such an attack, but this is false. Braddock marched with great caution, with the proper advanced guards and flanking parties:

> Braddock's advance was cautious and conducted in good order. His pioneers, or combat engineers, hacked a twelve-foot-wide path through the virgin forest. The French watched the advance, but were reluctant to attack such a strong, well-organized column. Neither were they sure that they could defend Fort Duquesne against such a force. (Todish, 21, 22)

A French and Indian force under the command of Captain Beaujeu went out from the fort to try and defeat the British force before it reached Fort Duquesne. They ran into the advanced guard under Lieutenant Colonel Gage, and the battle was on. The French and Indians forced Gage to retreat to the main body of troops, and began to sweep around the sides of the army, firing behind cover, while the British troops stood out in the open. After a horrific battle in which Braddock was mortally wounded, the British were forced to retreat. Even though the British advanced with a strong, alert column, the French, firing from cover on the flanks, won the day for France and saved Fort Duquesne for the time being.

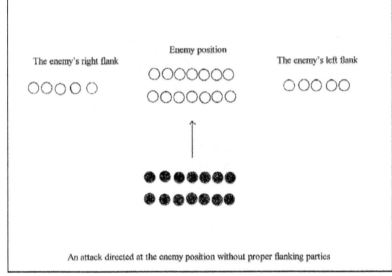

Figure 28.

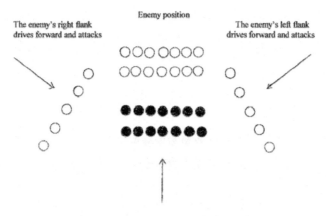

Rogers Rules #8

The enemy has retreated and taken up positions on a rising piece of ground
Their pursuers attack the center without regard to their flanks

Enemy position

The enemy's right flank
drives forward and attacks

The enemy's left flank
drives forward and attacks

The attack directed at the center, without flanking parties, is
overwhelmed by the attacks from the enemy's flanking parties

Figure 29.

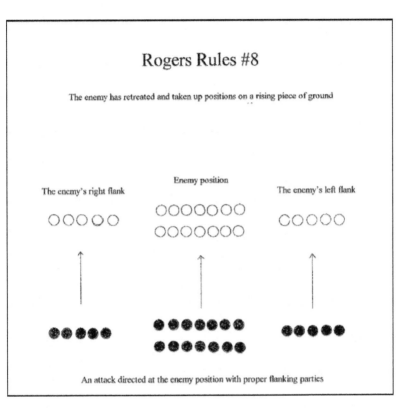

Figure 30.

Rogers' Rules: Number Nine

If you are obliged to retreat, let the front of your whole party fire and fall back, till the rear hath done the same, making for the best ground you can; by this means you will oblige the enemy to pursue you, if they do it at all, in the face of a constant fire.

(Rogers, *Journals*, 58)

As in Rule Number Seven, Rogers stressed the need to maintain a constant fire against the enemy; the difference is, in Rule Number Nine it applies to when the Rangers were forced to retreat from their enemy. This method of retreating—keeping half of the party loaded and holding their fire in reserve, while the front half fired and fell back—had been in practice for many years.

In 1724, John Lovewell of Dunstable, Massachusetts, petitioned the General Court in Boston for funding and permission to raise a group of volunteers to attack the Abenaki Indians in retaliation for many raids against frontier settlements. Permission was granted, and Lovewell was commissioned captain of his volunteer force. Thirty men soon enlisted, partly to try to stem the tide of Indian attacks, but also for the bounty money paid for Indian scalps. Lovewell and his volunteers raided into Indian territory and came back with Indian scalps, which made them heroes to the frontier families who had suffered attacks by the savages in the past. New volunteers enlisted readily whenever Lovewell and his men took to the field in search of Indians. In April of 1725, Lovewell organized a party of forty-six men to begin a scout along the Merrimack River in search of Indians. Reduced to thirty-six men due to illness and other circumstances, they met up with a war party of eighty Pigwacket warriors under the leadership of the war chief, Paugus. In the ensuing battle at Saco Pond, (now called Lovewell's Pond) the Indian party forced the Massachusetts men to retreat, which they did while keeping a constant fire against their attackers:

> Presently the scouts could see that the Indians were trying to surround them, and they began a fighting retreat toward the pond, giving up ground slowly in the direction of Fight Brook. As they continued to retreat, they gave up ground that held the bodies of their dead, but the fight was so intense that the Indians were unable to take any scalps. The English were trying to reach a place near the shore where winter ice had pushed up a small barrier of rocks and earth. (Kayworth/Potvin, 149, 150)

The fire of the retreating scouts must have been very intense if it prohibited the Indians from being able to stop and scalp the dead. The French were also paying bounties for English scalps, so this is a good indication of the stiff resistance that the scouts directed against their enemy.

The small barrier at the water's edge was only a temporary shelter, and the outnumbered men, having lost their commander (Lovewell was shot in the first volley and died a little while later), knew that they would have to continue their fighting retreat to a better defensive position. Without a place to give them a chance to regroup and make a stand, the men from Dunstable were doomed. The surviving men eventually fought their way to back to Fight Brook, and found a good piece of ground to make their stand. The natural terrain of the area helped the men defend themselves:

> Framed by high swamp grass and rushes where it met the water, the wide sand bar held scattered pine trees and a few fallen trees that might serve as breastworks. If Wyman (Seth Wyman, with all their officers killed, rallied the remaining

men) and his men could get to the fallen trees, the swamp could protect their right flank. (Kayworth/Potvin, 150)

These remaining men, badly outnumbered, desperately needed a strong place to rally to and defend. They had lost more than a third of their company, and the swamp protecting one of their flanks was a godsend for the little force, which could not be stretched any thinner to guard both flanks. The use of a constant fire while retreating, and making for the best ground possible to give your party an advantage, served the remnants of Lovewell's party well. In the ensuing battle, Chief Paugus was killed, and the rest of the natives gave up the fight in the face of heavy casualties.

Captain Lovewell and many of his New England snowshoe men were seasoned bush fighters, the same type of men that a young Robert Rogers would meet when he was a militia volunteer along the Merrimack River. These veteran Indian hunters were his mentors, and no doubt, Rogers learned much from these men. Rogers' Ranging Rules mirror many of the tactics used by these early Rangers.

Some British officers began to advance the need for irregular tactics. James Wolfe wrote down a list of instructions for the 20th Regiment of Foot prior to the beginning of the French and Indian War:

> These little parties are to keep their posts till the enemy attack with a superiority; upon which they are to retire to some other place of the same kind, and fire in the same manner, constantly retiring when they are pushed. (Todish/Zaboly, 78)

James Wolfe, promoted to Major General for the campaign against Quebec, had a dim view of the usefulness of the Rangers when he first came to America, but after he participated in the siege of Louisbourg where he witnessed the effectiveness of these men, he actually requested companies of Rangers for his army when it sailed for Quebec.

George Augustus, Lord Viscount Howe, as mentioned earlier, was also instrumental in the adaptation of irregular tactics into the British Army:

He (Howe) was responsible for many modifications in the Regular soldier's dress and tactics to better adapt to North American conditions. While some of these changes were already being undertaken before Howe arrived in America, his enthusiastic support of them, and his personal example in practicing them, makes him the Regular officer most commonly associated with these adaptations. (Todish/ Zaboly, 70)

At the "Battle of Bloody Run," which occurred during Pontiac's siege of Fort Detroit on July 31, 1763, Rogers and a handful of his Rangers went out with a British force made up of members of the 55th, 60th and 80th Regiments, under the command of Captain James Dalyell. This force sallied out of Fort Detroit to try to attack the Indians in a show of force, to cause them to lift their siege. The Indians had gotten word of this assault and were lying in ambush at a bridge the British would have to cross near Parents Creek. The Indians sprang their trap as the column began to cross this bridge. The troops had been ordered to fire by "street firings" if attacked by the enemy.

Lieutenant-General Humphrey Bland describes the method of "street firings" in "The Duty of the Officer and Soldier," found in the 1759 edition of his *Treatise of Military Discipline*:

It is so called from your being obliged to engage in a street, high-way, lane or narrow passage, where no more than ten, twelve, sixteen, or twenty files, can march in front; so that, according to the breadth of the place, your platoons must be stronger or weaker. (Bland, Chapter 6, 97)

General Bland originally wrote this military manual in 1727, to reflect changes he felt could be incorporated into the tactics being used by the British Army at that time. A new standardized military musket was being developed, and the tactics and manual exercise needed to be reformed to make use of this new weapon. Over the next few years, subsequent editions of Bland's manual simplified some of the maneuvers used by the army, so that some of the steps were shortened or eliminated. Author and Ranger historian Tim Todish explains street firings in his *Annotated and Illustrated Journals of Robert Rogers*:

Street firing was a technique used in narrow and confined areas. The soldiers were formed in a column, with a designated number abreast. The front flank would fire a volley, then fall back to the rear of the column and reload. The next rank would then fire and fall back to reload in the same fashion. The other ranks would do likewise, resulting in an almost continuous volley being directed at the enemy. This could be done from a stationary position, or while advancing or retiring, and was a very effective tactic. (Todish/Zaboly, 285)

It must be remembered that this system of firing was intended and developed for the use of Regular troops, but the similarities between Rogers' methods in Rules Number Seven and Number Nine are apparent. Rogers, again, did not invent many of the ideas he used for his Ranging Rules, but he adapted them to suit the Rangers' methods of woodland warfare.

At the Battle of Bloody Run, a fierce fight broke out at the bridge, with the Indians fighting under cover and the darkness of the night (the march had begun at 2 a.m.). The Regulars, unable to bring the attackers to close combat, were forced to retreat under heavy casualties, which included Captain Dalyell. This fighting retreat, which was probably done using the "street firing" tactic, as the troops were crowded together on the bridge and the road leading up to it, was done in fairly good order. Major Rogers had taken command of a house after driving a force of French and Indians out of it, and by diverting the attackers' attention from the main body, covered their withdrawal, even though the Rangers were in danger of being cut off because of doing this. Rogers' men fortified the house with bales of furs, and boards ripped from the roof. They held off repeated assaults against the house until two rowboats came up the river, which fired upon the enemy with a three-pound cannon that was carried in the bow of the first ship. Rogers and his men were able to escape back to Fort Detroit under the cover of the two rowboats, and their own fighting retreat. The Indians under Pontiac were eventually forced to lift the siege of Fort Detroit.

This method of maintaining a constant fire against the enemy, while trying to reach a defensive position, turned retreats that could been disasters into orderly withdrawals upon which the enemy could not press their advantage. Again, the excellent marksmanship skills of the Rangers were of the utmost importance in maintaining this constant fire. If the individual Rangers could not hit their picked targets, these firings would have done little to stop the enemy from pressing the Rangers as they retreated.

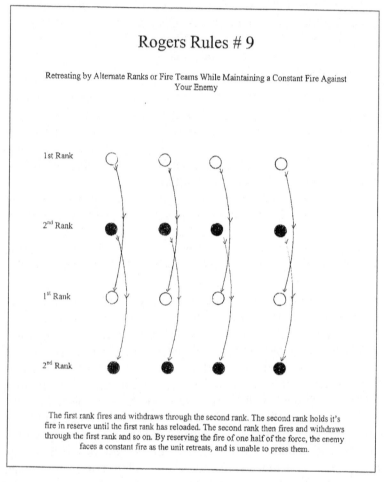

Figure 31. Retreating by alternate ranks while maintaining a constant fire.

Rogers' Rules:
Number Ten

If the enemy is so superior that you are in danger of being surrounded by them, let the whole party disperse, and every one take a different road to the place of rendezvous appointed for that evening, which must every morning be altered and fixed for the evening ensuing, in order to bring the whole party, or as many of them as possible, together, after any separation that may happen in the day; but if you should happen to be actually surrounded, form yourselves into a square, or if in the woods, a circle is best, and if possible, make a stand till the darkness of the night favors your escape.

(Rogers, *Journals*, 58, 59)

As we have discussed previously, Rogers and his Rangers conducted their scouts and raids deep into French-held territory. The Rangers not only had to slip past the French troops and their native allies, but the local inhabitants as well. They were in constant danger of encountering an enemy scout or being cut off from their retreat. The Rangers scouted past Fort Carillon (Ticonderoga) to Fort St. Frederick at Crown Point many times. If they were discovered in the area and the alarm was sounded, the

Rangers would have to get past the French troops, who would be out in force trying to catch the Rangers before they slipped by them on their way home. This actually happened to the Rangers when they were on a scout to Crown Point and intercepted some French troops traveling upon the frozen lake in horse drawn sleds. Some of the sleds were able to escape, and raced back to Ticonderoga to sound the alarm. The Ranger group was now caught between two French strongholds, from which troops and Indians could sally out in pursuit of the Rangers. The Rangers started their march back, and were ambushed by a large party of French and Indians. A fierce battle began with the Rangers forming a front and beating back repeated attacks on their flanks and center. The Rangers suffered many casualties, and with their ammunition running low, Rogers called for a different bit of strategy to save what remained of his force:

> After the action, in which we had a great number so severely wounded that they could not travel without assistance, and our ammunition nearly expended, and considering that we were near to Ticonderoga, from whence the enemy might easily make a descent, and overpower us by numbers, I thought it expedient to take the advantage of the night to retreat, and gave orders accordingly. (Rogers, *Journals*, 40)

Rogers and his men were in danger of being surrounded by a superior force. The French could be reinforced with fresh troops from Ticonderoga or Crown Point, and if their supplies or ammunition ran low, they could get more from either of their forts quickly and easily. If the Rangers stayed put, and their ammunition ran out, the French and Indians would have massacred or captured the whole party. Rogers used any advantage that he could to get his men back safely, and this time he used the cover of night to hide his retreat from the enemy. This tactic was not a new one, and had been used by a group of French and Indians in 1689, when a raiding party under the command of Francois Hertel attacked the settlement at Salmon Falls, New Hampshire, and made off with 54 captives. On his way back to Canada, Hertel's war party ran into a group of 150 New England militiamen near the Wooster River:

Hertel's son was badly wounded in a firefight that caused heavy casualties on both sides. Hertel managed to escape under the cover of darkness and he continued north with his captives. (Kayworth/Potvin, 101)

As these frontier stories about Indian fighting were told over the years, we can have no doubt that a young Robert Rogers listened intently, and learned a few lessons that would serve him well, later in life. Remember that these early Rangers were his woodland teachers. In his introduction to his *Journals*, he attests to the fact that he constantly sought knowledge from the area's hunters and trappers:

Rogers suggests that he early on developed an insatiable curiosity about the outlying areas he had not yet visited. Some descriptions of these lands he "received from Indians, or the information of hunters." (Todish/Zaboly, 28)

Rogers traveled over much of the frontier on his own, where he learned the "haunts and passages of the enemy." A clear knowledge of the surrounding area would give him a definite advantage in his Ranging pursuits.

Rogers told his men, when they were forced to scatter, to do it singly, "with each man taking a different road." Many men, each retreating by a different path, would be much harder to track than one big group withdrawing together. The darkness of the night would also help to hide the movements of a single man better than a small group of men. Rogers also appointed a place of rendezvous each morning, so his men would have a set place to retreat to in case of their being broken in a fight. The men could then regroup and rally, or continue their retreat as circumstances dictated. This tactic saved the lives of many men that night, and was something he had done in the past when on a scout to Crown Point early in the war. The Rangers were trying to capture a prisoner for intelligence, but could not procure one, so they killed twenty-three head of cattle, of which they feasted on the tongues before beginning their march home. During their return march, they almost ran into a large party of the enemy:

We at this time discovered eleven canoes manned with a considerable number of French and Indians crossing the

lake directly towards us, upon which we retired; and the
better to escape our pursuers we dispersed, each man taking
a different route. We afterwards assembled at the place
where we concealed our packs, and on a raft crossed over to
the west side of the lake. (Rogers, *Journals*, 15)

Rogers would use this tactic of appointing a place, or several
places of rendezvous, to meet at if the Rangers were forced to
scatter, or other circumstances caused the party to be separated
during the day. On one scout a Ranger almost perished because of
accidentally becoming separated from the rest of the men:

We then set out on our return, and arrived at Fort William-
Henry the 18th instant, except one man, who strayed from
us, and did not get in until the 23d, then almost famished for
want of sustenance. (Rogers, *Journals*, 18)

It has been said that this Ranger had returned to where he had
left his pack by mistake, and lost the rest of his party. He was out
another five days after Rogers and the rest of the party returned.
He was no doubt out of provisions, save what he could get from
nature, for most of this time. Rogers and his men had to be ever
vigilant when in the enemy's territory, always on the lookout for
the slightest hint of trouble:

The 23rd we marched eight miles, and the 24th six more,
and then halted within 600 yards of Carillon fort. Near the
mills we discovered five Indian's tracks, that had marched
that way the day before as we supposed, on a hunting party.
On my march this day between the advanced guard and the
fort, I appointed three places of rendezvous to repair to, in
case of being broke in an action, and acquainted every
officer and soldier that I should rally the party at the nearest
post to the fort, and if broke there to retreat to the second,
and at the third to make a stand till the darkness of night
would give us an opportunity to get off. (Rogers, *Journals*,
66)

This is a prime example of Rogers' caution when scouting the
enemy. He knew that there was a party of Indian hunters out in the
area, and they could possibly come across the tracks of his party.
The alarm would be sounded, and the French would be scouring

the countryside for the Rangers. He prepared the men for the possibility of an attack, and arranged his orders for a well thought out retreat to several places, where they would make a stand until darkness allowed them to escape. Even with the men scattering, and each taking a different route to the next rallying point, the Rangers still conducted an orderly retreat, with clear orders, and a plan for escape under the cover of darkness.

We have already discussed the Indians' tactic of trying to surround an enemy force and decimate their ranks by firing at all sides from the safety of the surrounding cover. Braddock's army, after Gage's advanced guard retreated to the main body, stood in tight groups of confused men, and tried to shoot at targets that were nothing more than the flash of a musket. At first, the British troops held their own against the French Regulars and Canadians, but the withering fire from the rear and sides by the Indians soon turned the tide of the battle:

> The Indians, encouraged, began to rally. The French officers who commanded them showed admirable courage and address; and while Dumas and Ligneris, with the regulars and what was left of the Canadians, held the ground in front, the savage warriors, screeching their war-cries, swarmed through the forest along both flanks of the English, hid behind trees, bushes, and fallen trunks, or crouched in gullies and ravines, and opened a deadly fire on the helpless soldiery, who, themselves completely visible, could see no enemy, and wasted volley after volley on the impassive trees. The most destructive fire came from a hill on the English right, where the Indians lay in multitudes, firing from their lurking-places on the living target below. But the invisible death was everywhere, in front, flank, and rear. The British cheer was heard no more. The troops broke their ranks and huddled together in a bewildered mass, shrinking from the bullets that cut them down by scores. (Parkman, 126)

This action was a prime example of the reforms that needed to be made in the British Army, to adapt to the new style of fighting that the woodlands of America would require. The Rangers were the direct result of early disasters like Braddock's defeat. To try and stand in close ranks, and fire volleys, only by the command of an officer, while your enemy hid behind cover, was foolish, but during the course of the war, the British command was unable to reply with an answer from their own ranks. The Rangers were the only true answer to the bush fighting techniques of the French and their Native allies. We can easily see how some of Rogers' Ranging Rules could have changed the outcome of this battle. The Rangers would have fought from cover, keeping enough distance between men to prevent multiple casualties from one shot. The Rangers' ability to maintain a constant fire against the enemy, instead of wasting fruitless volleys, would have kept the Indians from pressing their advantage along the flanks and rear of the column. With concentrated firepower from behind cover, the Indians would have soon realized that the party could not be overcome, and possibly ended their attack, or at least stopped long enough to regroup, which would have given the Rangers time to push back at the Indians, or rally themselves at their present position.

Rogers and his Rangers were themselves in danger of being surrounded at the site of their worst defeat, "The Second Battle on Snowshoes":

> This threw their whole again into disorder, and they retreated a third time; but our number being now too far reduced to take advantage of their disorder, they rallied again, and made a fresh attack upon us. About this time we discovered 200 Indians going up the mountain on our right, as we supposed, to get possession of the rising ground, and attack our rear; to prevent which I sent Lieutenant Phillips, with eighteen men, to gain the first possession, and beat them back; which he did, and being suspicious that the enemy would go round on our left, and take possession of the other part of the hill, I sent Lieutenant Crafton, with fifteen men, to prevent them there; and soon after desired two gentlemen, who were there volunteers in the party, with a few men to go and support him, which they did with great bravery. (Rogers, *Journals*, 78)

Rogers, badly outnumbered, used his reserve forces judiciously to prevent his party being surrounded, but had lost so many men in this action, that the enemy could press him repeatedly on all sides. The enemy would eventually be able to break one of his flanks and surround his party:

> The enemy pushed us so close in front, that the parties were not more than twenty yards asunder in general, and sometimes intermixed with each other. The fire continued almost constant for an hour and a half from the beginning of the attack, in which time we lost eight officers and more than 100 private men on the spot. We were at last obliged to break, and I with about twenty men ran up the hill to Phillips and Crafton, where we stopped and fired on the Indians who were eagerly pushing us, with numbers we could not withstand. Lieutenant Phillips being surrounded by 300 Indians, was at this time capitulating for himself and party, on the other part of the hill. He spoke to me, and said if the enemy would give them good quarters, he thought it best to surrender, otherwise he would fight while he had one man left to fire a gun. (Rogers, *Journals*, 78, 79)

Rogers and his remaining men were in a desperate situation. Lieutenant Phillips surrendered under the promise of good treatment from the Indians. Rogers had lost many men killed and wounded to enemy fire. The Ranger commander was in great danger of losing his entire force, and his own life as well. Rogers ordered his remaining men to scatter, using different routes back to Lake George, and then on to the place they had hidden their sleds:

> I now thought it most prudent to retreat, and bring off with me as many of my party as I possibly could, which I immediately did; The Indians closely pursuing us at the same time, took several prisoners. We came to Lake George in the evening, where we found several wounded men, whom we took with us to the place we had left our sleds. (Rogers, *Journals*, 79, 80)

Critics of Rogers have said that he ran away on this occasion, leaving many of his wounded behind to face the wrath of the French and Indians on their own, but when you study Rogers and his Rules, you soon learn that nothing could be further from the truth. Rogers merely acted with the common-sense style of the New Hampshire frontiersman, the same common sense that governs most of his Ranging Rules. By retreating, he saved what few men survived this encounter.

Rogers also revealed the formation he felt best suited to repel the enemy if surrounded. The use of a square formation, or if in the woods, a circle was best to prevent the enemy from breaking your order. In this formation you could hold off attacks until the cover of darkness might enable you to escape. The Osprey book, *American Colonial Ranger The Northern Colonies 1724-64*, by Gary Zaboly shows the circle formation with reserves held in the rear, that the Rangers used during the "Second Battle on Snowshoes" This is plate D, with the color plates starting after page number 32.

Colonel Henry Bouquet also advocated the use of a square formation during his expedition against the Ohio Indians. Colonel Bouquet did not think it was a good formation for marching through the woods, but in the event that the party was surrounded, with no hope for retreat, he thought it best for a defensive formation. The Reverend William Smith describes the possible need for a circle or square formation when under attack in his treatise of the Bouquet Expedition:

> He must therefore think of a retreat, unless he can force his way thro' the enemy. But how is this to be effected? His baggage and provisions are unloaded and scattered, part of his horses and drivers killed, others dispersed by fear, and his wounded to be carried by soldiers already fainting under the fatigue of a long action. The enemy, encouraged by his distress, will not fail to increase the disorder, with redoubled fury and savage howlings. He will probably form a circle or square, to keep off so daring an enemy, ready at the least opening to fall upon him with the destructive tomahawk: but these dispositions, thro' a tolerable shift for defense, are neither proper for an attack, nor a march thro' the woods. (Todish/Zaboly, 258, 259)

Colonel Bouquet used the following method to form the square to receive the enemy:

The whole halt to form the square or parallelogram, which is done thus. The first two men of the center column stand fast at two yards distance. The two men following them, step forward and post themselves at two yards on the right and left. The others come to the front in the same manner, till the two files have formed a rank, which is the front of the square. The rear face is formed by the two file-leaders turning to the center road, where having placed themselves at two yards distance, they face outwards, and are followed by their files, each man posting himself on the right or left, and facing towards the enemy the moment he comes to his post. As soon as the front and rear are extended and formed, the two long faces, who have in the mean time faced outwards, join now the extremities of the two fronts, and close the square. (Todish/Zaboly, 265)

Of course, these movements would have to be performed with speed and with precise maneuvers, with an enemy who knew their best advantage would be to attack before you had time to form the square or circle. The Rangers would have moved themselves into position much more quickly than these Regular troops. We must remember that Rogers trained his men to react with lightning quickness when given an order, and this quickness would have been essential in this situation. This speed, combined with his clear and concise orders about retreating, and how to form the men if surrounded, saved many a life throughout the French and Indian War.

Rogers' Rules:
Number Eleven

If your rear is attacked, the main body and flankers must
face about to the right and left, as occasion shall require,
and form themselves to oppose the enemy, as before
directed; and the same method must be observed, if
attacked in either of your flanks, by which means you will
always make a rear of one of your flank-guards.

(Rogers, Journals, 59)

In Rule Number Eleven, Rogers repeated some of the advice of
his previous rules. Rule Number Six described how to form a
front when marching in large numbers, keeping proper flanking
parties to the left and right of the front. Rogers stressed
strengthening the flanks to prevent the enemy from overcoming
the sides of the formation. Similarly, Rule Number Eleven
describes how to deal with an attack upon the rear of the party.

As we have discussed before, Rogers always tried to instill in
his men the need for constant caution and readiness for any
eventuality. Because they scouted deep into enemy territory, the
chance of pursuit by the enemy after a strike was almost
inevitable. As before advised, the Rangers would have marched in
a single file while keeping out their advanced guards and flanking
parties, but they also would have kept a strong rear guard in the
back of their file. With such a strong possibility of pursuit, this

rear guard would have to be extra cautious in their protection of the rear of the Ranger formation. Attacks on the rear of files or columns were common. After raiding parties left their targets, pursuit often began as quickly as a group could gather their gear, provisions and firelocks.

In February of 1693, A French force attacked three Mohawk villages in New York:

> Governor Frontenac equipped a force of about four hundred regulars and militia and two hundred mission Indians to move against the Mohawk towns. The expedition under Mantet and Courtemanche, appeared suddenly on February 8 and burned three villages. Although the warriors were out hunting, the French took about three hundred prisoners and destroyed the tribe's food supplies. All this pillaging required several days, and Albany got word promptly. Major Ingoldsby procrastinated, seeking more militia before he would march. Finally Peter Schuyler set off on February 13 with two hundred seventy-five whites and about as many Indians, and caught up with the invaders four days later. He started a running fight that cost the French between thirty and eighty killed and many wounded. Moreover while defending themselves on the move, they lost most of their Mohawk captives. (Peckham, 46)

Even with their slow start, this group of rescuers saved many lives by pursuing the war party. Indian attacks on the frontier were frequent, and many villages suffered multiple attacks. Deerfield, Massachusetts, devastated by raids in 1676 and 1694, suffered another attack in February of 1704:

> On the last night of February, 1704, a mixed party of two hundred Canadians and a hundred and forty Abenakis and Christianized Indians of Caughnawaga attacked. They were under the command of Captain Hertel de Rouville, veteran of the last war. (Peckham, 63)

This force killed many of the inhabitants and set fire to several houses before retreating into the night with one hundred and eleven captives, many of them women and children. The need to act quickly was critical, because the French and Indians would likely kill any captives that could not keep up with them in their retreat:

> The surviving villagers pursued the retreating raiders and inflicted thirty casualties but lost nine more of their own people without recovering any of the captives. (Peckham, 63)

Rogers knew pursuit was always likely after one the Rangers' raids, so he trained them to be able to meet an attack from the rear, forming quickly to repel the enemy force. Rogers instructed the main body to face about, and with the rear guard, form a front to confront the enemy. The flanking parties faced about to the right and left respectively, and maintained their positions to protect the flanks of the main body. By doing this, the right flank became the left, and the left became the right flank. The rear guard then became the advanced guard, and the advanced guard maintained the rear guard position. This tactic could also be used if the attack came against one of the flanks. The direction of attack determined how the men would be formed to meet the enemy. If attacked on the right flank, that party combined with the main body of troops and formed the front, while the left flank became the rear guard. The advanced guard became the left flank and the rear guard became the right flank. By merely facing about, the Rangers could quickly turn and face the enemy attack, and still maintain their flanking parties and rear guard. An attack could come from any direction, so the ability to react quickly and change the formation to present a strong front and flanks to the enemy was critical.

Parties of French and Indians pursued Rogers and his command of Rangers, Provincials, and Regulars after they attacked the Indian village at St. Francis in late 1759. Rogers and the rest of his men tried to make their way back home by way of the Connecticut River, because a party of French and Indians had discovered the boats and provisions they had left for their return trip. With this party already on their trail, and the survivors of the St. Francis attack sure to spread the alarm of the Rangers being in the area, the force had to retreat as quickly as possible. The Rangers faced a long march through a vast wilderness with few provisions. During this march, when their food began to run out, Rogers separated his force into smaller groups at Lake

Memphremagog. He reasoned that smaller parties might find game more easily. A party under the command of Ensign Avery fell victim to one of the French pursuing parties:

> After nine days travail in an unknown Wilderness...[we] were at the close of the Ninth day surprised by a party of Indians about Twenty or Thirty in Number that had pursued us & watching an opportunity when we were resting our Selves being much Enfeebled by travail & destitute of provisions save mushrooms & Beach Leaves for four or five days then past Came upon us unperceived till within a few foot of us. (Todish/Zaboly, 175)

It is interesting to note that the French and Indian party did not merely attack the rear of this party, but waited until they could capture them at rest. The Rangers normally would have posted their guards and picked a spot from which to make a stand, but in this case many were barely able to stand up, let alone put up any resistance.

The detachment under the command of Captain Dalyell at the "Battle of Bloody Run" was attacked in the rear of their column, after the initial ambush at the front of the British Force. The rear of the column was under the command of Captain Grant, and received a vigorous fire from the enemy:

> Captain Grant, being in the rear, was now likewise fired on from some houses and fences, about twenty yards from his left, upon which he faced about his own and Captain Hopkin's company, and gave a full discharge upon. (Todish/Zaboly, 279-284)

By quickly facing about and giving the enemy a severe fire, Grant's and Hopkin's men were able to drive the enemy from their places of ambush, and take possession of the fence and houses.

The expedition under the command of Colonel Bouquet against the Ohio Indians used a similar tactic to break through the group of Indians that besieged them at the "Battle of Bushy Run." Bouquet ordered two companies of troops to act as if they were retreating, in hopes that the Indians, thinking the army was collapsing, would come out from their hiding places and pursue the retreating troops. According to Reverend Smith:

The savages gave entirely into the snare. The thin line of troops, which took possession of the ground which the two companies of light foot had left, being brought in nearer to the center of the circle, the barbarians mistook those motions for a retreat, abandoned the woods which covered them, hurried headlong on, and advancing with the most daring intrepidity, galled the English troops with their heavy fire. But at the very moment when, certain of success, they thought themselves masters of the camp, the first two companies made a sudden turn, and sallying out from a part of the hill, which could not be observed, fell furiously on their right flank. (Todish/Zaboly, 234)

This feigned retreat, along with the sudden turn about by the first two companies, totally surprised the pursuing savages, who thought they would be falling upon a scared and disorganized group of men, instead of a resolute and disciplined force. The Indians fought back at first with some success, but a second charge by the British troops put the natives to flight. The victorious troops posted themselves in such readiness that the remaining Indians did not try any further attacks against the formation. The British Army, after so many years of combat, was beginning to understand how to deal with the Indians in their native environment.

Quick decisions and even quicker reactions were necessary as the Rangers confronted the enemy. Rogers' concern for his men and their safety was evident in all his rules by the attention that he focused on their vigilance and actions, even during retreat. The Rangers prepared themselves for an attack from any direction, and were able to form themselves quickly to withstand it.

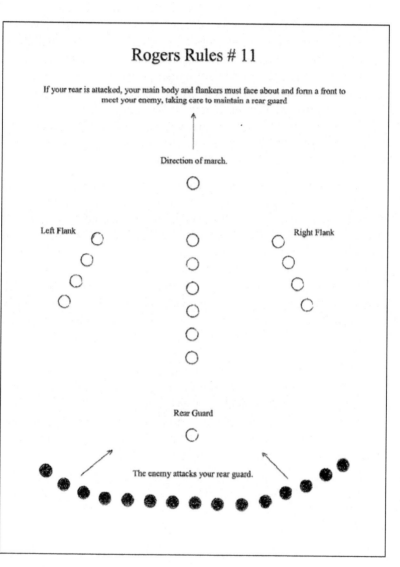

Rogers Rules # 11

If your rear is attacked, your main body and flankers must face about and form a front to
meet your enemy, taking care to maintain a rear guard

Direction of march.

Left Flank

Right Flank

Rear Guard

The enemy attacks your rear guard.

Figure 32.

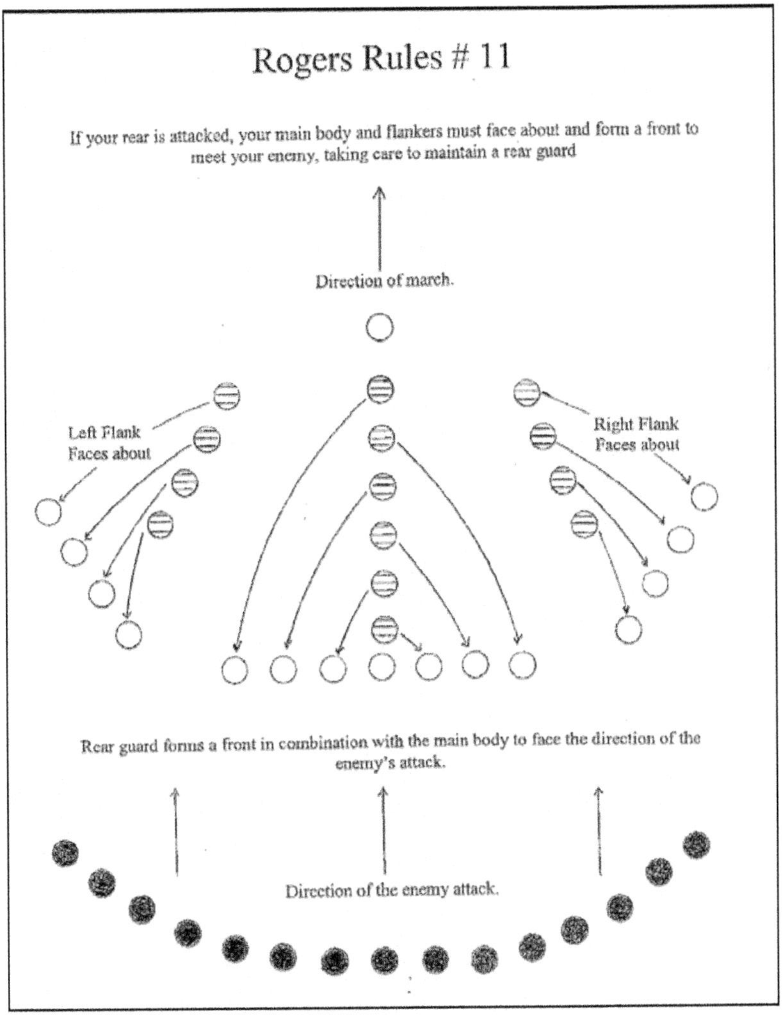

Rogers Rules # 11

If your rear is attacked, your main body and flankers must face about and form a front to meet your enemy, taking care to maintain a rear guard

Direction of march.

Left Flank
Faces about

Right Flank
Faces about

Rear guard forms a front in combination with the main body to face the direction of the enemy's attack.

Direction of the enemy attack.

Figure 33.

Rogers' Rules: Number Twelve

If you determine to rally after a retreat, in order to make a fresh stand against the enemy, by all means endeavour to do it on the most rising ground you come at, which will give you greatly the advantage in point of situation, and enable you to repulse superior numbers.

(Rogers, *Journals*, 59)

Almost any other group of fighting men, when in retreat, would only be thinking of escape from their enemy, but this was not the case with Rogers and his Rangers. Even in retreat, Rogers thought about how his forces could turn and go back on the offensive, even when confronted by a superior force hot on their trail. He trained his men to use any advantage possible to make their escape, or to turn the tables on the French and their allies.

Repeatedly in his rules, Rogers stressed the need to make a stand on "rising ground." This higher position naturally worked against the enemy. The exertion of charging up a slope would affect the attackers' ability to shoot at the Rangers or return their fire. A breathless soldier, his lungs heaving from running up a hill, would have great difficulty aiming and firing his weapon accurately.

Most marksmen agree that it is far easier to hit a target by shooting down at it, as opposed to shooting uphill. It would also be much harder for the enemy to see the formation of the defenders waiting at the top of the hill, while the defenders would easily see the direction of attack and movements of the enemy. If the enemy attempted to work their way around the flanks of the Rangers, the defenders would see them and send men to the side to stop this movement. These defensive movements would be hidden from the enemy, who again, would not be able to see maneuvers made on the top of the mountain or hill.

The decision to rally and make a stand against the enemy would of course be contingent on the belief that the Rangers could withstand an attack, especially if they were outnumbered. The best example we have of the use of Rule Number Twelve is the attack on the French woodcutting party within shouting distance of Fort Carillon (Ticonderoga) on March 7, 1759. (We previously used this battle as an example of the Rangers' tactics in Rule Number Three.) Rogers and his men came upon a party of about forty French troops cutting wood along the south edge of Lake Champlain. The Rangers attacked the party in complete surprise, killed many of them, and took several prisoners. The survivors of the attack retreated in the direction of Fort Carillon. A force of eighty Canadians and Indians sallied out of the fort in pursuit of the Rangers, with 150 French Regulars close behind. Rogers and his men began a retreat in the face of this superior force (Rogers' command consisted of about ninety men). Three times the Canadians and Indians attacked Rogers' force, but each time the Rangers' use of "rising ground" held the attackers at bay:

> About eighty Canadians and Indians pursued us closely, being backed by about 150 French regulars, and in a mile's march they began a fire in our rear; and as we marched in a line abreast, our front was easily made; I halted on a rising ground, resolving to make a stand against the enemy, who appeared at first very resolute: but we repulsed them before their reinforcement came up, and began our march again in a line abreast; having advanced about half a mile further, they came in sight again. As soon as we could obtain an advantageous post, which was a long ridge, we again made a stand on the side opposite the enemy. The Canadians and Indians came very close, but were soon stopped by a warm fire from the Rangers and Mohocks. They broke

immediately, and the Mohocks with some Rangers pursued, and entirely routed them before their Regulars could come up. After this we marched without any opposition. In these several skirmishes we had two Rangers and one Regular killed, and one Indian wounded, and killed about thirty of the enemy. (Rogers, *Journals*, 119, 120)

Rogers' force took advantage of the terrain and natural pieces of rising ground to rally and repel the Canadians and Indians who were rushing after them. This was done so quickly that the force of French Regulars in support of the Canadian and Indian attackers did not have time to come up and enter into the engagement before the Rangers had driven off the attacking force. When the Rangers gained the high ground on the long ridge, Rogers stationed his men on the opposite side of the ridge, so they could rise up and surprise the enemy with an unexpected volley.

In addition to judicious use of the terrain, the Rangers' firepower and marksmanship helped drive off their attackers. When Rogers wrote to Lord Loudoun in October of 1757 and explained his "Ranging Rules," he commented on the use of a volley to better his situation in retreating:

I would retreat with my flanking parties out, and whenever the ground gave me the advantage, I would improve it by firing a volley at them, which ground I should be very carefull to look for in order the better to defend and Secure our retreat. (Rogers, *Rising Above Circumstances*, 195)

Rogers must have had a lot of confidence in his Ranging Rules, and his men's ability to carry them out. Going on the offensive—even when retreating from a superior force—placed a great deal of pressure on his men. They had to react quickly, as we discussed before, and they had to use the terrain and their firepower to drive off their pursuers.

Rogers used many of his previous rules in combination with Rule Number Twelve. We can be sure he would have kept half his force loaded and in reserve when the Mohawks and some of his Rangers rallied and charged the enemy from the top of the ridge. If his whole force had charged down the ridge, we can be reasonably sure that they pursued the enemy under a constant fire, by advancing alternately while one rank reloaded, and the other covered them. Most probably, Rogers would have left a party in reserve at the top of the elevated position, in case the enemy regrouped, rallied, and pushed back against the pursuing Rangers. Rogers and his men would always be on the lookout for good, advantageous pieces of ground to rally to, and make a stand in their retreat; just another good example of the common-sense style of Rogers and his frontier Rangers.

Rogers' Rules: Number Thirteen

In general, when pushed upon by the enemy, reserve your fire till they approach very near, which will put them in the greatest surprize and consternation, and give you an opportunity of rushing upon them with your hatchets and cutlasses to the better advantage.

(Rogers, *Journals*, 9, 60)

As stated before, the Rangers liked to shoot a combination of a round lead ball with several lead shot, the "size of full grown peas." This would have been a particularly potent load at close range. Imagine the carnage that a concentrated volley would inflict on a group of men trying to scramble uphill against a defensive position. As discussed in Rogers' Rule Number Twelve, the Rangers marched to an elevated position, and made a stand on the other side of a ridge when pursued by a party of Canadians and Indians after ambushing a party of French woodcutters at Ticonderoga. The Rangers, who popped up from the other side of the long ridge they were hiding behind, held their fire until the pursuers were at close range, then drove them off, killing about thirty of them. This concentrated volley would have been against individual picked targets, as opposed to just firing in mass like the tactics of Regular troops. Half of the Ranger force waited in reserve, muskets loaded, in case the first volley failed to stop the attackers. The Rangers' expert marksmanship proved deadly to many of their enemies.

While the enemy was confused and disoriented, Rogers urged his men to rush forward and finish them off with hatchets and cutlasses. Here we are introduced to a new weapon, the cutlass. Use of the hatchet and tomahawk as a weapon and tool by the Rangers was discussed in Rule Number One, with Rogers dictating that his Rangers appear each night at roll call with one, but so far no references have been found regarding the use of swords by the Rangers. Officers may have worn them, but they were probably of a finer make, and may not have been suited for use in the woods. The use of swords for frontier militia companies and groups of Rangers or "snowshoe men" is well documented in the late 1600's on up to the mid 1700s. The colony of Massachusetts directed the following orders for members of the militia in the late 1600s:

> Every listed souldier…shall be always provided with a well fixed firelock musket, of musket or bastard musket bore, the barrel not less then three foot and a half long, or other good firearms to the satisfaction of the commission officers of the company, a snapsack, a coller with twelve bandeleers or cartouch-box, one pound of good powder, twenty bullets fit for his gun, and twelve flints, a good sword or cutlass, a worm and priming wire fit for his gun. (Massachusetts militia laws, Nov. 22, 1693)

New Hampshire had similar laws for militiamen:

> Every soldyer Shall be well provided w'th a well fixed gun or fuse, Sword or hatchet, snapsack, Catouch box, horne Charger & flints. (New Hampshire militia laws, Oct. 7, 1692)

A cutlass is a heavy short sword with a slightly curved single edge blade. These weapons are normally associated with sailors or naval troops, who used them on board ships, where their strong, short blades were better suited for battles upon cramped ships decks. The accompanying photo shows the actual sword carried by Benjamin Church. Benjamin Church commanded a company of militia during "King Philip's War," 1676-1677. His company was made up of a combination of white New England men and loyal Native Americans. Church purposely mixed his company, so that the whites could learn the Indian methods of fighting. Church was a strong proponent of adopting the natives' tactics into the New England militia companies, in order to fight the French and Indians during this time period.

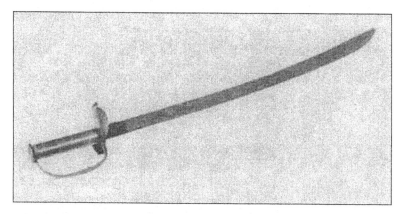

Figure 34. Benjamin Church's sword.

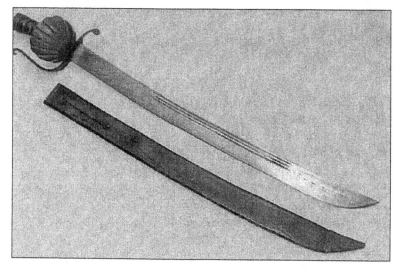

Figure 35. A reproduction naval cutlass.

These short, heavy blades would have worked well in the woods, where the ability to swing a long sword may have been compromised by the trees or brush. The sight of a group of Rangers screaming over the top of a ridge and brandishing hatchets and cutlasses, would have had a great psychological effect on the attacking Canadians and Indians after receiving a devastating volley.

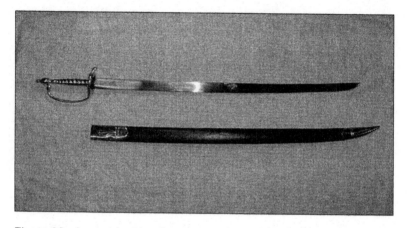

Figure 36. A reproduction of a 1742 British "hanger" or short sword. You can see the similarities between this sword and the reproduction cutlass. This sword, with its 25-inch long blade, is of the style that was worn by British Regulars and Grenadiers, although infantrymen were usually ordered not to wear them on the field.

In late 1757, two Rangers charged with stealing rum were whipped for this infraction, then thrown in the guardhouse. As we discussed before, whippings were rare among the Rangers, as opposed to being a common occurrence among Regular troops. Rogers was a careful disciplinarian, using the whip only when necessary. The Rangers did not care for this type of punishment, which they considered appropriate only to Regular troops, not Rangers. A whipping post was set in the ground in the Ranger encampment on Rogers Island. On the evening of December 6, a group of Rangers gathered around the whipping post and began complaining about its use for the Rangers. As the group's anger grew, so did their fury to revolt. One of the Rangers grabbed a nearby ax and quickly cut down the whipping post. The angry mob then attempted to free two Rangers being held in the guardhouse.

When they could not open the door, they began to tear the boards off the guardhouse roof. Ranger Captain Shepard, hearing the commotion, came running to investigate what was happening. Seeing the revolt taking place, and knowing that he needed to stop it, Captain Shepard called for the Rangers to turn out and stop the men from tearing down the guardhouse:

> Captain Shepard came running. One man pointed a musket at him, but Shepard knocked it aside with his sword and snatched it. (Cuneo, 63)

Captain Shepard eventually was able to stop the revolt and disperse the mob. This reference gives us an example of the use of a sword by a Ranger. When Captain Shepard heard the commotion, either he grabbed his sword, or he was already wearing it. This goes along with the Rangers always being ready for any eventuality or trouble, ready to react at a moment's notice.

It is interesting to note that Rogers mentions using the hatchet or cutlass, but not a bayonet, when falling upon the enemy after a close volley. European military tactics of the eighteenth century relied on mass volleys followed by bayonet charges to attack their foes, especially after the development of the socket bayonet. The socket bayonet allowed the soldier to fire and reload his firelock with the bayonet fixed. In Rogers' Rule Number One, and in Captain John Knox's description of the early Rangers in Nova Scotia, the hatchet is mentioned as a standard weapon or tool of the Ranging companies.

Did the Rangers use bayonets? When General Amherst ordered Rogers and his Rangers out to attack the French fortification at St. John in mid 1760, he gives us a clue as to the use of bayonets by the Rangers:

> You will take your men as light with you as possible, and give them all the necessary caution for the conduct, and their obedience to their officers, no firing without order, no unnecessary alarms, no retreating without order; they are to stick by one another and nothing can hurt them; let every man whose fire-lock will carry it have a bayonet; you are not to suffer the Indians to destroy women or children, no plunder to be taken to load your men, who shall be

rewarded at their return as they deserve. (Todish/Zaboly, 199)

General Amherst gave these orders in late May of 1760. Rogers and his force set out on this mission in early June. We can learn a lot about bayonet use by the Rangers from these orders. This was very late in the war, but many of the Rangers must still have been carrying personal weapons such as hunting fusils and some rifles. We know this is the case from the General's orders that "every man whose firelock will carry it is to have a bayonet." This confirms that some of the Rangers were carrying weapons that would not accept a bayonet, such as the before mentioned fusils and rifles. This also confirms that some of the Rangers were using military weapons that accepted a bayonet. At this late stage of the war, if they had not already been issued bayonets, the use of the bayonet by the Rangers must have been minimal.

The guerrilla-style of warfare practiced by the Rangers probably influenced them to prefer the hatchet or the cutlass to the bayonet. This also influenced the *way* the Rangers used these weapons. The hatchet, cutlass and bayonet all would have served the same purpose as a weapon, but since the Rangers wanted to travel as light as possible, they probably only carried one of these items. A Ranger would not carry a hatchet *and* a bayonet, or a bayonet *and* a sword. The hatchet's usefulness as both a weapon and a tool probably caused it to be carried more often than the bayonet or sword. If the Ranger was using a personal firelock that wouldn't accept a bayonet, this was a moot point anyway. A Ranger with a firelock that did not accept a bayonet would have used the hatchet or cutlass in place of the bayonet.

The practical use of a weapon would have been more important to the Rangers than any other factor. The ability to travel light and use one item for multiple purposes fits the style and tactics of the Rangers. Again, these are only assumptions, based on historical references as to the tactics and methods of the Rangers. Hopefully we may some day uncover concrete evidence to support the overall use of the bayonet by the Rangers.

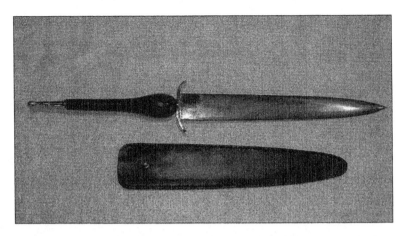

Figure 37. A reproduction "plug bayonet" and scabbard. Part of its versatility is that it can double as a knife, but as the name implies, when the wooden handle is inserted into the barrel of the musket, it "plugs" the barrel, so the musket cannot be fired when the bayonet is inserted, or "fixed."

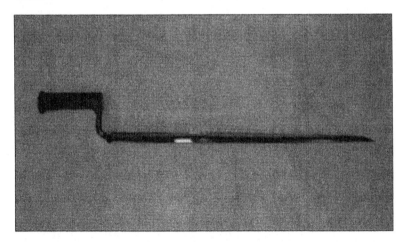

Figure 38. A reproduction "socket bayonet." This style allowed the musket to be reloaded and fired, while the bayonet was fitted onto the barrel of the musket. This style of bayonet, when combined with a standardized military musket, greatly changed the military tactics used in the eighteenth century.

Rogers' Rules: Number Fourteen

When you encamp at night, fix your centries in such a manner as not to be relieved from the main body until morning, profound secrecy and silence being often of the last importance in these cases. Each centry therefore should consist of six men, two of whom must be constantly alert, and when relieved by their fellows, it should be done without noise; and in case those on duty see or hear anything, which alarms them, they are not to speak, but one of them is silently to retreat, and acquaint the commanding officer thereof, that proper dispositions may be made; and all occasional centries should be fixed in a like manner.

(Rogers, *Journals*, 60)

We have already discussed the type of ground the Rangers preferred when making an encampment, as well as the need for making this camp after night had fallen. Making the camp under the cover of darkness helped the Rangers avoid detection, and prevented the enemy, if watching, from being able to see how the men were disposed in case of attack. Rogers also wanted these encampments to be made on a piece of ground that would give the sentries the advantage of seeing or hearing the approach of the enemy, so that they could warn the party of this danger.

Rule Number Fourteen addresses the positioning of these sentries in order to avoid being surprised and possibly having the camp overrun by the enemy. Rogers stressed the importance of silence in the camp. Any unusual noise in the woods would be a beacon to an enemy in the area. Once, in mid-1756, the Rangers, traveling in whaleboats upon the lake, were passing Ticonderoga when they heard the call of a French sentry:

> The following evening we embarked again, and went down the bay to within six miles of the French fort, where we concealed our boats till the evening. We then embarked again, and passed by Ticonderoga undiscovered, tho' we were so near the enemy as to hear the centry's watch-word. (Rogers, *Journals*, 18)

The need for strict silence when operating in enemy territory is illustrated by the fact that the Rangers were able to pass by undetected, while the French gave away their positions with unnecessary noise.

If the sentries became aware of the approach on the enemy, one of the men was to silently move from the lookout position and return to the main camp, where he would quietly give the information to the commanding officer. The sentry would relay critical information such as the number of the opposing force and the direction from which they were approaching. This would help the commanding officer decide how to form the men for a possible attack, or even to decide that a retreat was better if the opposing force was far superior in numbers. By sending only one man, the remaining men on sentry duty would still be able to watch the movements and approach of the enemy, and would frequently convey updated information to the main party. One man's movements in the dark of night would be less likely to be seen than the movements of the whole party of six sentries. The number of men Rogers assigned to sentry duty also gives us some ideas of how the Rangers operated when out on their scouting missions. We can get a pretty close idea of the amount of time that these men would be separated from the rest of the party, which also gives us an approximate idea of how long the Rangers would rest at night.

We know that Rogers directed his men to march until dark before setting up their encampment for the night. At times these marches continued until early morning. As we will learn in a later rule, Rogers also expected his Rangers to be awake and ready to move before first light. We can conclude from these factors that the amount of rest time during these encampments would be from six to nine hours, with six hours probably being closest to the actual time spent on watch duty. Therefore, a six-man sentry, with two men awake and alert at all times, would change every two hours. This shorter time on watch would be easier on the men, and would lessen their chances of falling asleep and being surprised. This small group of men would only be relieving each other, lessening the amount of noise and movement required when doing so. These men were separate from the main body so that what movements they had to make would not draw attention to the rest of the party.

To operate in the enemy's territory while leaving the camp unguarded was to invite disaster. The scalp-hunting party under the command of Captain John Lovewell in 1725 fell into an Indian ambush because of leaving their packs unguarded:

> John Lovewell then issued an order that ultimately proved to be catastrophic. He ordered the men to lighten their load by leaving their blanket rolls and knapsacks in a pile on the ground. For some inexplicable reason, in those risky circumstances, Lovewell decided to leave the bulk of their food and supplies unguarded! This was the same man who routinely sent out scouting parties to reconnoiter the trail ahead, and who periodically dispatched scouts on his back trail to avoid being ambushed. (Kayworth/Potvin, 141, 142)

Lovewell and most of his men were seasoned bush fighters, who were usually very cautious when scouting into Indian Territory. A party of natives under Paugus found their unguarded packs, and set up an ambush for the Rangers when they returned to retrieve them. Lovewell was not the type of man who normally made mistakes like this, especially when out hunting scalps.

Earlier in the year, when out on another Indian hunting scout, he had his party leave their packs behind, but left them well guarded:

> We traveled 6 miles and came upon the tracks of Indians, and we left 16 men with our packs and the rest pursued the tracks till dark that night and staid there all night, and on the 17th we followed their tracks till about 8 o'clock. (Kayworth/Potvin, 142)

Even when sentries were posted, if they were not diligent in their duties, the enemy could still penetrate their encampments. The Rangers were particularly good at getting past the French guards by crawling through their sentries.

> "Early on the 28th about ten in the morning came in view of an Encampment at the lower end of the Lake at the Carrying place, of about one thousand French and Indians – We crawled thro' their Guards to within thirty or forty rods of the Encampment." (Hall, 37)

A rod is measurement used by eighteenth-century surveyors. They used chains to do their surveying work:

> The common unit of surveying measurement in the eighteenth century was the chain. One chain is equal to: 66 feet, 100 links, 4 rods, and 4 perches. Therefore, 1 mile is equal to: 80 chains or 120 rods or perches. (Todish/Zaboly, 242)

A rod would be one quarter of a chain, or sixteen and one-half feet. If the Rangers crawled to within thirty rods of the French encampment, this meant they were approximately 495 feet away from the main force of the enemy. To have crawled through the French guards, to within 500 feet of a party of 1000 French and Indians, tells us how skilled the Rangers were on their reconnaissance missions. This practice of crawling through the French guards to spy on their encampments was a tactic the Rangers used frequently:

> There was no Fort or Artillery there. We retired & went about one mile & a half further, & discovered their Grand Encampment – Crept thro' their guards to within Sixty rods, found a Fort building there – discover'd a Number of

Cannon Mounted – we had a convenient Situation for a View, which we kept till toward night & by the appearance of the Tents & Troops, French & Indians we judged likely to be about three thousand. (Hall, 37)

This vital information turned out to be the building of the French Fort Carillon at Ticonderoga. The Rangers would visit this strategic post many times during the early years of the war.

Not all scouting parties met with the same success in their missions into French territory. A scout under the command of William Symes, who was captain of another Ranger company in Blanchard's New Hampshire Regiment, experienced some trouble when they did not post their sentries in the proper manner. This scout was sent out from Gen. William Johnson's camp at Lake George in pursuit of intelligence of the French forces after the "Battle of Lake George":

> "Monday ye 13th Instant Set out from ye Camps about 2, o'the Clock in ye afternoon upon Comd with fifty men under my Command Travild about three miles upon ye West of ye Lake and sent out 3 Scouts according to orders; and Encamped 2 of which Performed their orders and return'd without any Discovery, but thro' mistake the officer was ordered for to send ye North Scout, sett only a Centry, who was Placed near 45 Rods from ye encampt and about half an Hour after sunset he was fired upon as near as we could by a Scout from ye Enemy Consisting of four or five Indians, Upon which I ordered all to arms and to proceed with all speed to ye place where ye fire was and when I got there to my astonishmt I had but about 15 men with me, I Looked Back and they Cried out for Gods sake call us all together or we shall be cut off." (Hall, 45)

The lone sentry was killed and scalped by the Indians, and it was reported that the Indians left a hatchet sticking in his head. The rest of the party scrambled about in fear and ran back to the camp, grabbing their packs to retreat from the death they were sure was at their backs. Captain Symes, with great difficulty, was able to keep the party at their encampment, but could not persuade the frightened men to continue on their ordered scouting mission. Unable to proceed, Symes had no choice but to return to the main camp at Lake George. The mistake of not posting enough sentries in the proper dispositions doomed this scout. A sentry consisting of six men, as Rogers would later specify in his rules, would have prevented the lone sentry being surprised and killed, and would have allowed the mission to be completed.

Rogers' Rules:
Number Fifteen

At the first dawn of day, awake your whole detachment; that being the time when the savages chuse to fall upon their enemies, you should by all means be in readiness to receive them.

(Rogers, Journals, 60)

Once again, Rogers instilled in his men the need for constant caution and preparedness for any surprise from the enemy. Throughout the early years of the American colonies, the Native Americans were known for their raids against frontier towns and settlements. One of the savages' favorite tactics was to attack at the break of dawn, when the village inhabitants were least expecting an attack:

> "They approach like foxes, fight like lions, and disappear like birds," said a Frenchman who'd seen Indians in action. Their favorite tactic was the ambush or predawn raid, when people are least watchful. The idea was to hit hard, kill quickly, and escape with prisoners while the enemy was still off balance. (Marrin, 24, 25)

In these early dawn attacks, the victims, roused from their beds and still in a sleepy stupor, would be unable to mount much of a defense. Many would be in their nightclothes and their weapons would probably not be ready at hand to repel their attackers. It would also take time for the villagers' eyesight to adjust to the predawn darkness, while the attacking war party would already have adjusted to the low light conditions. Sometimes these towns were caught unaware because they had not posted any guards to spread the alarm in the event of a surprise attack.

In the late 1600s and early 1700s, the predawn raid was used to great effect by the French and their Native American allies. The massacre at Deerfield, Massachusetts, which we have discussed before, was conducted in the predawn darkness. This attack became one of the most famous raids of "Queen Anne's War":

> In the cold darkness of February 29, 1704, Reverend John Williams was jolted awake by shouts and the sound of his front door caving in under the blows of axes. Automatically, his head still fuzzy with sleep, he grabbed a pistol and aimed it at a figure near his bed. Luckily the gun misfired. His target was an Indian chief whose death would have meant death for Williams's entire family. The chief belonged to a raiding party of 250 Frenchmen, Abenaki, and Caughnawaga, Christian Mohawks who had moved to Canada from New York. They had traveled all the way from Montreal on snowshoes, buffeted by gusty winds that took away their breath. On the day before the attack, they reached the forest on Deerfield's outskirts. Numb with cold and fatigue, but not daring to make a fire for fear of being seen, they scooped burrows in the snow, lined them with spruce bows, and tried to hide from the wind. Luck was with them. Toward morning they were able to climb into the village without being seen, thanks to the windblown snow that had piled against the stockade. They took Deerfield quickly, although not before losing 40 men. (Marrin, 51)

The raids against Schenectady, New York and Salmon Falls, New Hampshire took place in the twilight of the morning. On February 8, 1690, attacking French and Indians wiped out Schenectady, and a month later fell on the town of Salmon Falls:

> The next month, another war party slipped out of the woods near Salmon Falls, New Hampshire. It was Schenectady all over again. This time thirty-four died and fifty-four were

taken prisoner. The captives–those who survived the horrors of the northward march–were held in Canada until their families or the colonial government exchanged them for ransom. (Marrin, 42, 43)

The French and their native allies were not the only ones to take advantage of the early morning while the enemies slept to attack. In early March of 1697, an Abenaki raiding party attacked the small settlement at Haverhill, Massachusetts. Hannah Dustin and her week-old baby were at home in the family cabin, while her husband and their other seven children were at work in their fields, when the war party attacked. Hannah's baby was snatched from her arms and smashed against a tree, killing it. After this quick raid, the Indians marched their prisoners off into the woods. After putting some distance between the settlement and their party, the Indians broke up into smaller groups with a few prisoners in each group, and began the six-week journey back to Canada.

The next six weeks were hell for the captives. Cold and hungry, their frostbitten feet bleeding, they were driven northward toward Canada. At night, while the Indians slept snugly around a campfire, they huddled on the fringes beyond its warmth. The Abenaki never tied them, because there was no place to run in the midst of the forest. Besides, the captives knew the penalty for trying to escape: slow death by torture. As they lay down on the night of April 29. Hannah whispered her plan to the others. She meant to kill their captors in their sleep. The sky was purpling in the east when the three whites rose and, finding tomahawks near a woodpile, stood over the sleeping figures. The grieving mother gave the signal. Ten times the tomahawks rose and fell, smashing into the Indians brains. All died instantly, except for a wounded Indian woman and boy who ran screaming into the woods. Calmly the whites scalped the corpses, took what supplies they needed, and headed for home. (Marrin, 48)

General James Wolfe used a predawn attack against the French guard posted at Anse du Foulon, or what is now known as "Wolfe's Cove." For weeks, Wolfe had tried to find a weak spot in Quebec's defenses in order to bring General Montcalm into the open and fight. One day while cruising on the St. Lawrence River looking for a place to land his troops, Wolfe made out a barely visible path leading up to the Heights of Abraham. From the size of the group of tents at the top, Wolfe figured that the guard there was small, and might be overpowered if the British troops could scale the rugged path and surprise them. Wolfe began a series of decoy maneuvers over the next several days to try to fool the French into thinking that his landing attempt would be below the town. These decoy movements worked, and Montcalm ordered his army to shadow the British Army as its ships cruised up and down the river as if they were looking for a landing place. This caused the French Army to be divided into many smaller units trying to keep up with all of the different maneuvers by the British. The guard posted at the top of Anse de Foulon consisted of one hundred men under the command of Captain de Vergor. Captain de Vergor was not a cautious man, and once had been tried for misconduct and cowardice. Vergor had allowed some of his men to go and work in their fields in exchange for working in his own. He also maintained a very loose watch, and he went to bed without ordering his men to continue shadowing the British troop movements above the town.

This was the opportunity Wolfe was looking for. A procession of British boats full of troops rowed down the river toward the French guard post:

> In a few moments they rounded the headland above Anse du Foulon. There was no sentry there. The strong current swept the boats of the light infantry a little below the intended landing place. They disembarked on a narrow strand at the foot of heights as steep as a hill covered with trees can be. The twenty-four volunteers led the way, climbing with what silence they might, closely followed by a much larger body. When they reached the top they saw in the dim light a cluster of tents at a short distance and made a dash at them. Vergor leaped from bed and tried to run off, but was shot in the heel and captured. His men, taken by surprise, made little resistance. One or two were caught, and the rest fled. (Parkman, 473)

By making his attack on the guard post in the early morning, Wolfe and his men were able to easily overpower the French troops at the top of the embankment. The British Army was able to march about a mile and assemble themselves three ranks deep, with their flanks and rear guards posted, before the French troops and General Montcalm even knew they had landed and taken command of the heights. The daylight raid had worked to perfection. The ensuing battle was a major defeat for the French, and the fortress city of Quebec fell a few days later.

The raid on the village of St. Francis is probably the best example of the Rangers using the Native Americans' tactic of the predawn raid against them. After their hardship-filled march to the St. Francis River, the Rangers formed a human bridge and crossed the river to the Indian village side. They slipped through the woods until they were in sight of the village. Rogers had his men make a stand, while he went forward to scout the village:

> Under cover of darkness, Rogers took Lieutenant George Turner of the Indian Company, and Ensign Elias Avery of Fitche's Connecticut Provincial Regiment to scout the town. They found that the Indians were engaged in a "high frolic or dance." At 3 o'clock in the morning, Rogers moved his men to within 500 yards of the town, deploying them on all sides to be sure none of the occupants would escape. They struck at the first light of dawn, catching the weary Abenakis by surprise. As they charged into the village, the Rangers saw "about six hundred scalps, mostly English" hanging from poles by the lodges. As the groggy Indians stumbled out of their dwellings they were shot, tomahawked, or bayoneted. Many of the Indians were trapped inside their burning buildings, making it impossible to get an exact count of the casualties. (Todish, 87)

Rogers' raid on St. Francis was a complete surprise and a total victory. Rogers understood the effectiveness of the pre-dawn raid. By having his Rangers awake and in readiness for an attack, he prevented their being surprised in the same manner. The St. Francis Raid illustrates some of the rules we have already discussed. The proper use of the ground insured that the Rangers could make a stand if attacked, and allowed the men to be positioned for the greatest advantage. Properly posted sentries prevented an attack. The Rangers could not afford to drop their guard for even a minute. Once again, Rogers' use of extreme caution, and doing absolutely everything possible to prevent being surprised, reveals the underlying tone of his "Ranging Rules."

Rogers' Rules:
Number Sixteen

If the enemy should be discovered by your detachments in the morning, and their numbers are superior to yours, and a victory doubtful, you should not attack them till the evening, as then they will not know your numbers, and if you are repulsed, your retreat will be favored by the darkness of the night.

(Rogers, *Journals*, 60, 61)

A s we have learned in many of Rogers' previous rules, the time of day, and the use of darkness as cover, is something Rogers recognized when making any tactical decisions, especially with the possibility of meeting a force superior in numbers. With the chances so great of being outnumbered when operating in enemy territory, the Rangers had to be very aware of when, and when *not* to attempt an attack or to push an advantage. The attack on the column of French and Indians at the "Second Battle on Snowshoes" is a good example of a superior force turning the tables on their attackers. Had the Rangers known that this column was only the advanced guard of a much larger French force, they could have allowed the party to pass by them, and then silently retreat. As it was, the much larger French force almost wiped out the entire Ranger scouting party, even though it cost them a considerable loss of men.

Rogers had allowed superior forces to pass by his undetected Rangers on numerous occasions. In December of 1755, the rangers were scouting in the direction of Ticonderoga, in search of a prisoner and the much-needed intelligence they could get about the enemy's strength and situation. The Rangers crept to within sight of the French, who were building a new fort. Rogers estimated this force to consist of about 500 men:

> By what I judged, the number of their troops were about 500. I made several attempts to take a prisoner, by way-laying their paths; but they always passed in numbers vastly superior to mine, and thereby disappointed me. (Rogers, *Journals*, 8)

Rogers and his men watched undetected as the French constructed the future Fort Carillon, but even with the advantage of complete surprise, Rogers still felt that the superior numbers of French troops passing him were not worth the risk of trying to attack them, or to take a prisoner. The 500 hundred French troops nearby were no doubt a big influence on Rogers' decision not to try to take a prisoner. If the ambush went badly, the 500 troops could have started a pursuit of the Rangers almost immediately after the alarm was sounded. To attack would have spelled disaster for the small Ranger patrol.

Rogers, however, was not averse to making a bold move against superior forces. In May of 1756, Rogers and a party of eleven Rangers were scouting towards Ticonderoga. After taking a good view of the French encampment from a nearby mountain (Rattlesnake Mountain, or what is now known as Mount Defiance), the Rangers spent the rest of the night on this perch. The next morning they marched to the Indian carrying place, or portage route, and set up an ambush between the fort and the French guard post:

> About six o'clock 118 Frenchmen passed by without discovering us; in a few minutes after, twenty-two more came the same road, upon whom we fired, killing six, and took one prisoner, but the large party returning, obliged us to retire in haste, and we arrived safe with our prisoner, at Fort William-Henry, the 23rd. (Rogers, *Journals*, 16)

The Rangers had to be extremely daring to allow a party of 118 Frenchmen to pass by, and then attack a smaller party just a few minutes later. The second party almost outnumbered Rogers' small group by two to one. Rogers must have been confident of their ability to attack the smaller party, take a prisoner, and then escape before the large party could turn the tables on them.

We have discussed how a predawn attack, using the cover of darkness and taking advantage of the unprepared condition of the enemy, can facilitate a successful attack.

Rogers had another use of the dark of night: that of hiding the number of his men when attacking a superior force. As the darkness helped to hide the Rangers' movements and allowed them to surprise the enemy, then the enemy would not be aware of the Rangers' true numbers, and they might assume they were being attacked by a superior force.

We know from our previous discussions that attacking during the darkness of night or the early morning hours was a very useful tactic, and could be accomplished in a variety of ways. Captain John Lovewell (whom we have discussed before) and a party of New England Rangers attacked a sleeping party of Native Americans on February 20, 1725. Although this party of Indians was not superior in numbers to the Rangers, we can still see the effectiveness of attacking the enemy at night:

> Once Lovewell's scouts had determined that the enemy had stopped for the night, he called a halt and waited for darkness. They shunned the comforts of fires that might betray their presence, and they waited through the long day for darkness to become their ally. At this point Lovewell demonstrated his skill as a bush fighter; he was methodical, stealthy, and cold blooded. In his quiet dispassionate way, he issued instructions to his men. By 2 a.m. he and his men had moved to within point blank range of the enemy encampment. Guided by his carefully worded instructions, they split into three groups and surrounded the campsite. The golden glow from a campfire bathed the silent arena with its dim light. The ten Indians lay close to the central campfire wrapped in blankets and furs and oblivious to the looming danger. The attack was executed efficiently according to Lovewell's plan. A ball from Lovewell's

musket triggered the assault and mortally wounded two sleeping warriors. A volley from the first reserve that killed five was followed by another volley from a second contingent that killed two more. The surviving brave started up from his sleep, but he too was dispatched when an attack dog jumped into the fray and prevented his escape. One can only imagine the scene that followed when the Rangers moved in to finish off the wounded and take the scalps; the incident can only be described as an execution or a massacre. (Kayworth/Potvin, 51, 52)

The darkness of night covering the numbers of Rangers attacking a party of the enemy was a definite advantage, especially if the Rangers were attacking a superior force. Most likely, the enemy would have just fallen asleep, or were fatigued from the day's activities and would be looking to get some rest. The confusion caused by a nighttime raid could prevent a larger force from putting up any kind of an organized defense, as well as creating great fear and a possible retreat.

During General Jeffery Amherst's siege of Fort Carillon in July of 1759, in a daring nighttime raid some French troops attacked a party of British troops guarding the trench works being dug towards the fort. The confusion produced by this attack possibly caused the deaths of some British troops by their own fellow soldiers:

During the night the enemy attacked our advanced guard of the trenches, by which we had lieutenant and four men killed, and eleven wounded: it is suspected that our people, in the first confusion, fired upon each other. (Knox, *Siege of Quebec*, 168)

The French resorted to more of these nighttime raids during the siege to retake Quebec in early 1760. After another battle on the Plains of Abraham, British forces under the command of Brigadier Murray were forced to retreat back behind the defenses of Quebec City by an attack from French forces under the command of General Levis. During the siege that commenced after this battle, some British troops were attacked in a nighttime raid:

We had an officer and twelve men advanced during the night of the 15th, under cover of a rising ground, beyond the blockhouse Number two; fifty French grenadiers, with a captain and two officers, crept upon them unperceived, and gave them a brisk fire; which our little party spiritedly returned, and fell then back to the blockhouse, lest they be surrounded: our officer lost three men, two of whom were scalped and otherwise barbarously butchered; the third was wounded and made prisoner, as we suppose. (Knox, *Siege of Quebec*, 257, 258)

The Rangers also conducted nighttime raids upon the French during the siege of Quebec by General Levis. The Rangers' ability to move quickly and silently proved to be a great advantage during these sorties against the enemy in the dark of night:

During General James Murray's 1760 battle with General Francois de Levis outside Quebec, Hazen's (Captain Moses Hazen of Rogers Corps,) Rangers experienced heavy fighting on the left wing of the redcoat army. The French won the day, pushing Murray's force back into the city. Posted outside the walls at night, the rangers skirmished with enemy partisans and raided the French trenches, just as Rogers' men had done during the siege of Fort Carillon in 1759. (Zaboly, *American Colonial Ranger*, 49)

In the event that a nighttime attack failed and his party was repulsed by the enemy, Rogers advised his men to use the cover of night to hide their retreat, no doubt using his earlier rule of each man taking a different route back to a rallying point, or place of rendezvous. Rogers and his Rangers used this tactic to withdraw from the battlefield at the end of the "First Battle on Snowshoes":

When darkness descended, Rogers called a council of war of his remaining officers, viz., Lieutenant John Stark, Ensigns James Rogers and Jonathan Brewer. "All officers were unanimous of opinion that it was prudent to carry off the wounded of [their] party and take the advantage of the night to return homeward, lest the enemy should send out a fresh party upon them in the morning, [besides, their] ammunition being almost expended [they] were obliged to pursue this resolution." (Loescher, vol. I, 133, 134)

The use of the cover of night to attack a superior force of the enemy, which may cause them to become confused and enable Rogers' Rangers to defeat them or force them to retreat, is typical of the Rangers' daring tactics. While many other units would have been reluctant to attack a superior force, a bold move like this was to be expected from the "Falcons of the Lakes." The ability to look past the initial attack and plan for a retreat under the cover of darkness, in case the enemy proved too strong or well prepared, was another trait of the Rangers: that of being prepared for any eventuality.

Rogers' Rules: Number Seventeen

Before you leave your encampment, send out small parties to scout round it, to see if there be any appearance or track of the enemy that might have been near you during the night.

(Rogers, *Journals*, 61)

Rule Number Fifteen directed Rogers' men to be awake and ready to receive the enemy at dawn, as that was when the Indians preferred to attack. In Rule Number Seventeen, Rogers took that rule a step further and applied it to breaking camp. Even if no dawn attack had occurred, the Rangers might have been discovered or spied upon. Rogers ordered small parties of men to search the area around the camp for sign that the enemy had been near them in the night. Most of the Rangers, raised on the frontier, were well versed in hunting and trapping, and the tracking abilities that went along with those pursuits. They were skilled at discovering and reading signs of the enemy:

> On July 31, a Fort Anne scout of 11 Rogers Rangers sent out from Half-way Brook came across the fresh tracks of 50 Indians. (Loescher, vol. II, 15, 16)

The ability to read different signs and tracks left behind by someone, or even something, could help prevent a surprise attack, or prevent the gathering of intelligence by the enemy. While in garrison at Annapolis, Nova Scotia, Captain John Knox gave some interesting descriptions of signs, or tracks left by the enemy:

> Six officers and a party of soldiers, all volunteers, amounting in the whole to thirty armed men, went out on 1 December to scour the country; as their route was through the orchards to the eastward of Mayass Hill, we took all the officers' servants and other men off duty, loaded them with apples, and sent them back to the fort; after which, the day being pleasant, we agreed to extend our walk and take a view of the country; we soon got upon the tracks of cattle, which we easily discovered by the snow upon the ground; and, when we had marched about five or six miles, we came upon human foot-steps: some of them had the impression of a moggasan or Indian slipper (moccasin, mockasin, molkasin, morgisson, mogasheen, mackassin, mocsen; in the New Hampshire provincial papers of 1704 the spelling is mockasin.) (Knox, *Siege of Quebec*, 53, 54)

Human footprints on the snow-covered ground were not the only way of telling how long ago the enemy had been at a certain location. Other signs could reveal this also:

> We also got upon the tracks of horses, and found some of their dung before it was cold, and afterwards some pieces of apples indented with human teeth which had not yet changed their colour; from these and other circumstances (needless to be recited) we had reason to think the enemy had discovered us, and were retired to one of their fastnesses: these are generally on a road or path by which they expect their enemy must pass; however still we marched on and, coming soon after upon fresh footsteps of men, we halted our party, animated our soldiers, and charged them not to suffer themselves to be surprised or terrified by shouts or yells: they promised, 'They would not yield an inch, but would stand by us like good soldiers.' (Knox, *Siege of Quebec*, 54)

By finding the dung from the horses, and it still being warm, the troops knew that the enemy had been there very recently. If you have ever eaten an apple, you know how quickly the leftover core starts to turn brown. These signs allowed the British party to prepare themselves for a possible ambush. After proceeding farther, the party came across more tracks, by which their guide determined that the enemy was waiting at a "very wicked pass," or a great place for an ambush. The party determined by this information, to return to the fort by a different route, and got back safely, without any other occurrences.

Parties of the enemy were constantly lurking around the areas surrounding the British or Ranger encampments, trying to take a prisoner or gain information. During General Amherst's advance against Fort Carillon at Ticonderoga in 1759, the French and their native allies were always lurking around the British Army, trying to cause whatever trouble they could:

> The French savages are daily skulking in the vicinity of our camp having the advantage of the adjoining eminences, whence they have a distinct view of all our transactions. (Knox, *Siege of Quebec*, 164)

When the British Army went into winter quarters at Quebec after its successful siege and taking of the city, the French kept parties of Indians out harassing the garrison and trying to attack and capture parties of woodcutters:

> A body of two hundred Indians are skulking about the country, between the garrison and our most advanced post at Lorette; Which is the cause of the governor's precautions respecting the wood-sleighers, who have a party of light infantry to cover them; and, in case of our being attacked, the eldest field-officer of the day is to sally out, at the head of the main-guard, to reinforce, and command the whole. (Knox, *Siege of Quebec*, 231)

The Rangers were extremely useful in guarding the British encampments from these roving bands of Indians and French partisans. During General Abercrombie's campaign against Ticonderoga in 1758, the British Army spent some time at their encampment at Lake George preparing from the coming advance up the lake. The army was well protected by the Ranger scouts.

While Abercrombie's army gathered in strength, Rogers Rangers were employed as usual in protecting the camp from surprise attacks. On June 16, "Orders were given for daily Scouts and Patrols being sent round the camp, through the woods…" This service was effectively executed and the army suffered no losses. (Loescher, vol. II, 7)

After the fall of Fort Carillon, Amherst set his sights on Fort St. Frederick at Crown Point. The Rangers again were employed in scouting and protecting the army. The Rangers were not always so successful in their efforts to protect the encampments of the advancing British Army. Small parties of French and Indians sometimes filtered through their defenses, despite the Rangers' best efforts:

Ticonderoga had finally fallen. No more would the bells of Carillon ring for French ears. Possessive eyes were now turned toward Crown Point. While Amherst waited for his bateaus to come up and be portaged to Lake Champlain he posted Rogers Rangers beyond the sawmills as a buffer between Ticonderoga and the partisan bands expected from Crown Point. The Rangers helped to obstruct the road to the lake to hamper the approach of a large force; but small raiding parties sifted through. On July 28, Ensign Jonas of the Stockbridge Company was peeling bark when he was killed and scalped. (Loescher, vol. II, 48)

Scalping was something practiced by both the French and British forces, with bounties being paid for enemy scalps as we have discussed before. Many of the British high command did not favor this practice, but did little to stop it:

If such commanders as General Abercromby considered scalping "a barbarous custom first introduced by the French, and of no use to the Cause" they rarely forbade their partisans from practicing it against the Canadians and Indians. (Zaboly, *American Colonial Ranger*, 47)

Figure 39. Two reproduction eighteenth-century knives. The top fixed blade knife is a copy of a common trade knife used by many of the Native Americans for scalping. The bottom knife is a copy of a common clasp knife, with horn slabs and brass bolsters, which was also used for scalping one's enemy.

These parties of Rangers who scouted around the British encampments were also in danger from their own fellow soldiers. On several occasions, British sentries mistook returning Rangers for the enemy:

On June 20, Sergeant Hartwell came into Fort Edward with his patrol. They were challenged by a British picket, but it being a windy night, they did not hear the guard's voice. He fired and killed Hartwell and the same hungry bullet passed through the stomach of the next Ranger. (Loescher, vol. II, 7)

The same type of accident, eerily similar, occurred just a few days later:

Sergeant David Kerr of Major Rogers' Company was returning to camp with his patrol on the evening of June 24th. He was likewise fired at and killed by a Regular sentry and the bullet also passed through another Ranger who recovered. (Loescher, vol. II, 7)

By waking his Rangers up before dawn, Rogers was able to have his men prepare for a possible morning attack. While these men made a stand, small parties were sent out around the camp to see if they could find any sign that the enemy had been near the camp in the night, which could provide much needed information to the Rangers before they began their morning march. If the Rangers found that they had been spied upon in the night, but not attacked in the morning, they could assume that the enemy might have fallen back to a better ambush site along the Rangers' intended march. The Rangers would know that the enemy knew they were in the area, and could then make plans to continue on their scout, return to their base, or change their destination. They could determine by the number of tracks whether the enemy was too strong to pursue, or to try to pass by them undiscovered.

The sign left by the enemy could also tell the Rangers that an enemy party had been near their camp in the night, but had not discovered them. The Rangers could then determine a course of action against this party, based on information gathered from the tracks or signs as to the size of the enemy party or the direction of travel.

Sometimes noise or other activity around the camp at night could prove to be something other than the enemy. During their march toward Saco Pond in 1725, John Lovewell's group of New England Rangers stopped for the night to rest themselves for the push against the Indian village:

> The march from Ossipe and the prolonged tension of being in the enemy's stronghold had tired the men, and after Lovewell assigned guards for the night, the off duty men welcomed the chance to catch up on their sleep. During the night, the guards thought they heard Indians prowling about the campsite. The sounds kept the company in a high state of alert throughout the night, but with the coming of daylight, they concluded the noise came from moose browsing in the small brook that entered the pond near their bivouac. (Kayworth/Potvin, 140)

You can almost feel the apprehension that these early Rangers felt, so close to the enemy's village, deep into their territory, and so very far from home. Rogers and his Rangers surely felt the same way at times. That is why any information that could be obtained from the enemy was so important. Not only did the Rangers practice the tactic of scouting around their own camps in the morning before marching, but they also performed this task for the British Army encampments as well, as we have previously discussed.

The Rangers performed many tasks that were different from those of the Regular soldiers. The Rangers' special abilities had a lot to do with the types of duties they were given.

> When encamped with the main army, The rangers' duties included making daily patrols beyond the perimeter, guarding workers on the road and in the woods, rounding up stray cattle, carrying mail and messages to other posts, apprehending deserters, and sometimes escorting provision wagon trains. Their status as a special force generally freed them from most of the drudge work of a typical military campaign, such as fort building, ditch digging, and rowing and poling supply boats. (Zaboly, *American Colonial Ranger*, 23)

These duties came with a tremendous amount of responsibility. If the Rangers did not perform these duties correctly and to the best of their abilities, the whole army would suffer. We can understand the importance of knowing if the enemy had been around the encampment during the night. Any movement by the Rangers or the army in the morning would hinge on this information. The Rangers' ability to read the tracks or signs left by the enemy was crucial to determine the enemy's number and direction of travel.

Rogers' Rules:
Number Eighteen

When you stop for refreshment, chuse some spring or rivulet if you can, and dispose your party so as not to be surprised, posting proper guards and centries at a due distance, and let a small party waylay the path you came in, lest the enemy should be pursuing.

(Rogers, *Journals*, 61)

At first it may seem strange that Rogers would give advice on how to stop for lunch. It is one more example of his constant caution and ability to think beyond the present situation.

The need to stop and eat or drink from time to time was very important to the success of the Rangers' scouts. The Rangers burned an enormous number of calories during their fatiguing missions. To replace these calories, periodic stops to eat and drink were part of the Rangers' routine, just as vital as many of the other tactics and methods they practiced.

Jeduthan Baldwin, a provincial captain, went on a scout with the Rangers in early 1756 and recorded the following:

March 11: Mchd. S.S.W. 18 miles & got to Ft. Wm. Henry abt. 2P.M., the men very weak & faint, having had nothing to eat for some time. (Todish/Zaboly, 43)

Figure 40. A reproduction eighteenth-century brass trade kettle. This is a common example of the type of cooking vessel used by many of the Ranger Companies, and was an important Indian trade item.

A tired and hungry Ranger would be less cautious, and more prone to make mistakes that could lead to capture or even death. A well-rested Ranger with a full belly would be much better prepared to meet anything the enemy could throw at him. The standard military ration for one week was:

> Seven pounds of beef, or, in lieu thereof, four pounds of pork, which is thought to be equivalent; seven pounds of biscuit bread [hardtack] or the same weight of flour; six ounces of butter, three pints of pease, half a pound of rice, and this is called seven rations. (McCulloch/Todish, *British Light Infantryman*, 26)

The Rangers, many of whom were excellent hunters, supplemented their rations with fresh game when they were allowed to hunt for it. Deer, elk, moose, and fowl were a welcomed substitute for their daily salted meat ration. Many of the Rangers carried lines and hooks in their packs, by which they took a variety of fish from the many lakes and streams in the area. Fresh fish complemented their otherwise bland, monotonous diet.

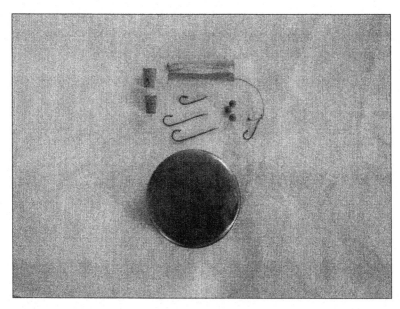

Figure 41. A reproduction fishing kit of the style that may have been carried by some of the Rangers. It includes linen fishing line wound on a wooden bobbin, forged fishing hooks, lead shot weights, corks for floats, and a small tin to carry them in.

Rogers suggests that the Rangers find a spring or small stream to rest beside when stopping to eat or refresh themselves. A source of water would be very important to men who exerted themselves as the Rangers did during their scouts. We have already discussed the sometimes difficult traveling conditions that the Rangers faced. Hot, humid weather would sap their strength in the summer, while the frigid cold and deep snow would be equally fatiguing in winter. Dehydration, even in the winter, is a great concern. Just before the Second Battle on Snowshoes, Rogers and his Rangers stopped for refreshment on their march, no doubt partially due to fatigue from snowshoeing in the deep snow:

> The 13th, in the morning, I deliberated with the officers how to proceed, who were unanimously of opinion, that it was best to go by land in snow-shoes, lest the enemy should

discover us on the lake; we accordingly continued our march on the west-side, keeping on the back of the mountain that overlooked the French advanced guards. At twelve of the clock we halted two miles west of those guards, and there refreshed ourselves till three, that the day-scout from the fort might be returned home before we advanced. (Rogers, *Journals*, 75, 76)

Figure 42. A reproduction French and Indian War era tin canteen, with a white rope cord for a shoulder strap, and a carved wooden stopper. Canteens and remnants of canteens have been found during archeological investigations on Rogers Island. The Rangers often mixed their rum ration in with their water to make what was known as "grog."

Officers expressed great concern regarding fresh water for their soldiers to drink. Soldiers were warned not to drink water from possibly tainted ponds or swamps. Lord Howe ordered that his men while marching:

"Should not be permitted to stoop to drink, as they are generally inclined to do, but obliged to lift water in their canteens, and mix ginger in it." (McCulloch/Todish, *British Light Infantryman*, 29)

Ginger was thought to be a good preventative against scurvy and dysentery. Even if the Rangers left on their scouts with full canteens, they would soon run out if they were drinking the proper amount of water during their travels. Modern Ranger reenactors know that they must constantly drink water during the day leading up to an afternoon battle reenactment, just to maintain a good level of hydration. That is why at many modern battle reenactments the officers and NCOs can be heard constantly telling their men to drink plenty of water. Each year many reenactors fall victim to heat exhaustion by not maintaining their water intake. The Rangers would have been no exception to this rule, and their level of exertion and loss of water would have been far greater than the small amount of time a modern reenactor is on the field at a historical event.

When Rogers was sent to accept the surrender of the western French posts after the fall of Montreal, he described the amount of game, types of timber, quality of the soil, and frequently, any good water sources that his party passed. Rogers very precisely described one large spring in his journals:

> On January 3d, south-east-by-east three miles, east-by-south one mile and a half, south-east a mile through a meadow, crossed a small creek about six yards wide, running east, traveled south-east-by-east one mile, passed thro' Indian houses, south-east three quarters of a mile, and came to a small Indian town of ten houses. There is a remarkable fine spring at this place, rising out of the side of a small hill with such force, that it boils above the ground in a column three feet high. I imagine it discharges ten hogsheads of water in a minute. (Rogers, *Journals*, 212, 213)

By the directions of travel Rogers gives in these journal entries, we can see the need for a good compass. Many of the places Rogers and his party traveled over were unmapped, and the descriptions and directions Rogers recorded would prove invaluable to future travelers and to the military.

Figure 43. A reproduction of the brass compass/sundial that was found on Rogers Island in the Hudson River across from the site of British Fort Edward.

Aside from the obvious need for a good, plentiful source of water along their march, another reason for the Rangers stopping to refresh themselves beside a small source of water soon comes to mind. We have discussed repeatedly the need for utmost caution when operating in enemy territory. Rogers listed tactic after tactic in his rules that helped prevent the Rangers from being surprised by the enemy when out on their scouts. Something as simple as stopping close to a source of drinking water is another example of this caution. If the Rangers stopped close to a good source of water, their movements around this temporary encampment would be kept to a minimum. If the Rangers stopped a large distance from the water source, the chance would be greater that the enemy might discover them when they went to the stream or spring for water. The least amount of movement would help the Rangers remain hidden.

Rogers mentioned stopping by streams, rivers or brooks three days in a row on his trip back from accepting the surrender of the French outposts, when encamping for the night:

On the 16th we marched nearly an east course about nine miles, and encamped by the side of a small river.

On the 17th kept much the same course, crossing several rivulets and creeks. We traveled about twenty miles, and encamped by the side of a small river.

On the 18th we traveled about sixteen miles an easterly course, and encamped by a brook. (Rogers, *Journals*, 216, 217)

We can see how much importance Rogers placed on stopping for refreshment or encamping by a source of good water, by its emphasis in his journals. Rogers again instructed his Rangers to post the proper sentries, disposed in the proper positions when stopping, even when it might be a quick stop for a cold meal. The need for some of the party to be on their guard while the rest of the men ate was critical to the safety of the group. An unguarded party would be easy to surprise and capture.

A party of French workers lost one man killed and scalped by the Rangers because they did not post their sentry properly. According to a French account of this Ranger scout in May of 1756, the whole party of twenty men could have been captured, but the report implies the Rangers ran away after killing the one man:

May 20, 1756. Agreeable to orders from the General, I set out with a party of eleven men to reconnoitre the French advanced guards. (Todish/Zaboly, 45)

This party of Rangers took a view of the work being done on the fort at Ticonderoga, and then set an ambush for any French work parties between the fort and the carrying-place. According to the Ranger report, they let a large party of French pass by, but then attacked a smaller group who passed by a few minutes later. The French account states that the French group was caught off guard, and totally surprised by the attack:

"At 9 o'c. of the morning, there arrived 13 men of the Canadian Militia, who escaped from the portage where they were attacked by some 15 English, as they say. It is true that M. de Beaujeu had ordered M. de Fortenay, cadet, to go there with 20 armed men, each one with an axe, to work on the portage trail. They left their arms at one end of the said portage with a sentry to guard them, and came to the other end to work there. This portage is ¾ of a league across. The English killed one man and scalped him, after which they left more promptly than they had come, without taking the trouble to follow the fleeing men; they could have captured these 20 men without firing a shot if they had wanted, as they were all sitting in a circle smoking their pipe." (Todish/Zaboly, 46)

French and English accounts during the French and Indian War tended to exaggerate the number of men involved, and they would definitely slant the report to look more favorable upon themselves. Whatever the case was here, we can see the mistake of leaving their arms so far away from where they were working, and then leaving only one sentry to watch over them. If the French were indeed sitting in a circle smoking their pipes, it would have been easy to surprise and attack them, with no sentries posted to watch over the resting men.

Caution was the watchword when it came to Robert Rogers and his Rangers. Rogers' journal contains many entries in which he kept out guards constantly to prevent being surprised, for example:

The 11th we proceeded as far as the first narrows on Lake George, and encamped that evening on the east-side of the lake; and after dark, I sent a party three miles further down, to see if the enemy might be coming towards our forts, but they returned without discovering any. We were however on our guard, and kept parties walking on the lake all night, besides centries at all necessary places on the land. (Rogers, *Journals*, 73, 74)

This journal entry shows how much concern and importance Rogers placed on the security of his camps. An unguarded encampment was an invitation for disaster. The French and their Indian allies taught a group of Rangers a lesson on caution during a scout in July of 1758:

On July 31, a Fort Anne scout of eleven Rogers Rangers sent out from Half-Way Brook came on the fresh tracks of 50 Indians. Following them for four miles the Rangers sat down to eat when they were surrounded and attacked by the

50 Indians. In the desperate melee 17 Indians and eight Rangers were killed. Two Rangers were taken alive and Sergeant Hackett alone escaped. (Loescher, vol. II, 15, 16)

Loescher does not list a source for this reference in chapter one, so we cannot be sure how the attack on this group actually happened, but if the Rangers did sit down to eat, they must not have posted any sentries, as almost the entire party was wiped out. It would seem strange that with the knowledge that there were fifty Indians in the area, close by from the signs they had left by their tracks, the Rangers would not have been on their guard and extra cautious. Whatever the case was, twenty-five men lost their lives, and two were captured; a real blow to the Ranger Corps. As the war dragged on, it became harder and harder to replace twenty-five good men. The number of available men from the colonial frontiers grew scarce, and some late-war Ranger recruits would not measure up to the early Rangers.

Rogers also advised his scouting parties to send a small party of men back on the trail that they came into their camp or resting place on, to set an ambush in case the enemy had discovered their trail and were following their track. This was another tactic that had been used by the early New England Ranger Companies. As discussed in a previous rule, Captain John Lovewell routinely sent scouts back on their trail to prevent being ambushed. Rogers used a variation of this tactic on his expedition against the Abenaki Indians of St. Francis, when he left two Indians on his back-trail to watch the Ranger's whaleboats:

Whaleboats and provisions against his return were cached in the underbrush. Early on 23 September the Rangers filed northeasterly into the wilderness, leaving behind two Indians "to lie at a distance in sight of the boats, and there to stay until I [Rogers] came back, except the enemy found them; in which case they were with all possible speed to follow on my track." (Cuneo, 104)

The French did happen to find Rogers' boats hidden in the brush, and began pursuing his track immediately. The two Indians left to watch the boat started after Rogers to warn him of this development:

In the evening of the second day of the march, the two Indians stumbled wearily into the rear guard. They had been running for many hours: some four hundred French had found and burned the boats; half were in hot pursuit of the Rangers. (Cuneo, 104)

The French also used a variation of this method of waylaying a back-trail after they found and destroyed the Rangers' whaleboats, by setting up an ambush at the site of the burned boats:

Rogers had reached the point of no return. His bridges were literally burnt behind him. Actually they were, for the French, after staving in the bottoms, burned the whaleboats that they did not take away. Bourlamaque swelled the pursuing party with 100 more men and increased the party posted in ambush near the charred whaleboats' ruins to 360 men to await the return of Rogers' command. (Loescher, vol. IV, 21)

Just as Rogers wanted his men to waylay the pathway behind them, the French forces wanted to be waiting in case the Rangers came back the way they had come, which until the two Indians reported that their boats had been discovered, was the Rangers' original plan. If the Rangers had not gotten this information, they may have fallen into the French trap on their way back home.

The ambush was a favorite tactic of both the French and their Native allies, as well as the Rangers. Waylaying their back-trail was just another way of setting up such an attack on their enemy. These ambushes could literally tear a group of men apart if well executed. The Rangers soon became particularly adept at this tactic of a surprise attack on the enemy from a concealed position. The French however, could play this game just as well:

"The work of Rogers' Rangers was often violent and dirty. Not infrequently did Robert Rogers find his best-laid plans going awry in the unpredictable and brutal arena that was forest warfare. Almost as often he found his own empirically-conceived Ranging rules failing him: on at least five different occasions during the war, Rogers led his men into enemy ambushes." (Todish/Zaboly, 93)

The nature of the ambush was something that the Native Americans had used to their advantage. These tactics were well suited to their hit-and-run style of fighting:

> Though an increasingly unfashionable word with some historians, there is no better one than "savage" to describe the nature of the forest combat the Rangers engaged in. (Zaboly, *American Colonial Ranger*, 47)

The Rangers not only fought as the Indians did, but some people suggest that they also adopted the appearance of Indians. Contemporary chronicler John Entick made this distinction between the look of the Rangers and the Light Infantry:

> The Rangers are a body of irregulars, who have a more cut-throat, savage appearance; which carries in it something of natural savages; the appearance of the light infantry has in it more of artificial savages. (Todish/Zaboly, 314)

Rogers' Rules:
Number Nineteen

If, in your return, you have to cross rivers, avoid the usual
fords as much as possible, lest the enemy should have
discovered, and be there expecting you.

(Rogers, *Journals*, 61)

This rule builds on the methods of setting and avoiding possible
ambush sites. Rule Number Eighteen instructed the Rangers to
send a small party back on the trail they marched in on, to possibly
ambush any enemy who might have discovered their tracks and
were now pursuing them. A good place to do this would have been
at the common fording places of the streams and rivers that had to
be crossed during a march or scout.

The colonial frontier was crisscrossed with many bodies of
water that could greatly hinder travel. The British Army's
expedition against Fort Duquesne, under the command of General
Braddock, was troubled in their march by the number of rivers and
streams they had to cross:

> Braddock consulted with Washington, who advised him to
> leave the heavy baggage to follow as it could, and push
> forward with a body of chosen troops. This council was
> given in view of a report that five hundred regulars were on
> their way to reinforce Fort Duquesne. Colonel Dunbar was
> left to command the rear division, whose powers of
> movement were now reduced to the lowest point. The

advance corps, consisting of about twelve hundred soldiers, besides officers and drivers, began its march on the nineteenth with such artillery as was thought indispensable, thirty wagons, and a large number of packhorses. "The prospect," writes Washington to his brother, "conveyed infinite delight to my mind, though I was excessively ill at the time. But this prospect was soon clouded, and my hopes brought very low indeed when I found that, instead of pushing on with vigor without regarding a little rough road, they were halting to level every mole-hill, and to erect bridges over every brook, by which means we were four days in getting twelve miles." (Parkman, 121)

Many of the soldiers of the French and Indian War could not swim. This, coupled with the amount of gear and weapons that they carried, made crossing any body of water a very dangerous undertaking. Eighteenth-century accounts of soldiers drowning fill the journals and orderly books of the French and Indian War period.

The Reverend William Smith recognized this problem in his account of the Bouquet expedition against the Ohio Indians. He felt that there was an easy answer to the way that soldiers could learn to cross deep water:

They ought to learn to swim, pushing at the same time their cloaths, arms, and, ammunition before them on a small raft. (Todish/Zaboly, 260)

Crossing rivers at a fording place was the safest way to get across these bodies of water. The Funk and Wagnall standard desk dictionary lists the following description of a "ford":

"A shallow place in a stream or river, that can be crossed by wading" or "to cross a stream at a shallow place."

Fording areas existed on many frequently crossed rivers and streams, where the water was normally shallow enough to traverse safely. The only problem with these fording places was that they provided a convenient opportunity for the enemy to prepare an ambush. These rivers would have to be crossed with the utmost caution and attention to the possibility of surprise attack:

The Braddock Expedition in 1755 was almost the victim of an ambush as it crossed the Monongahela River on the way to attack Fort Duquesne. Braddock, in order to bypass another natural ambush area, was forced to place his army in danger in two other places in order to avoid one:

> It was not till the seventh of July that they neared the mouth of Turtle Creek, a stream entering the Monongahela about eight miles from the French fort. The way was direct and short, but would lead them through a difficult country and a defile so perilous that Braddock resolved to ford the Monongahela to avoid this danger, then ford it again to reach his destination. (Parkman, 121)

The French and their native allies were shadowing the movements of Braddock's Army, and they soon would have figured out his intended route and the need to ford the river twice. The French, with their knowledge of the river and the surrounding countryside, would have tried to ambush the British force at one of those fording places:

> It was near one o'clock when Braddock crossed the Monongahela for the second time. If the French made a stand anywhere, it would be, he thought, at the fording-place, but Lieutenant-Colonel Gage, whom he sent across with a strong advance-party, found no enemy, and quietly took possession of the farther shore. (Parkman, 124)

French Captain Beaujeu, with a force of 900 mixed French, Canadians, and Indians, planned to ambush the British force at this ford, but delays cost him this point of surprise:

> Why had not Beaujeu defended the ford? This was his intention in the morning; but he had been met by obstacles, the nature of which is not wholly clear. His Indians, it seems, had proven refractory. Three hundred of them left him, went off in another direction, and did not rejoin him till the English had crossed the river. Hence perhaps it was that, having left Fort Duquesne at eight o'clock, he spent half the day in marching seven miles, and was more than a mile from the fording place when the British reached the eastern shore. The delay, from whatever cause arising, cost

him the opportunity of laying an ambush either at the ford or in the gullies and ravines that channeled the forest through which Braddock was now on the point of marching. (Parkman, 124, 125)

We have discussed Rogers' use of the terrain, the darkness of night and early morning, and countless other means to ensure the safety of his men and the success of his missions. By not using the usual fording places on the rivers the Rangers would have to cross, Rogers was helping his scouting parties to avoid a possible ambush at these well-used sites. Many of the Rangers were expert trackers and were accustomed to life on the edges of civilization, therefore they were able to find other safe crossing places that enabled them to continue their scouts. Many enemy ambushes were prevented by this Ranger tactic of avoiding a pattern of crossing at the same places. This is just another simple yet very important example of how the Rangers faced their woodland enemies.

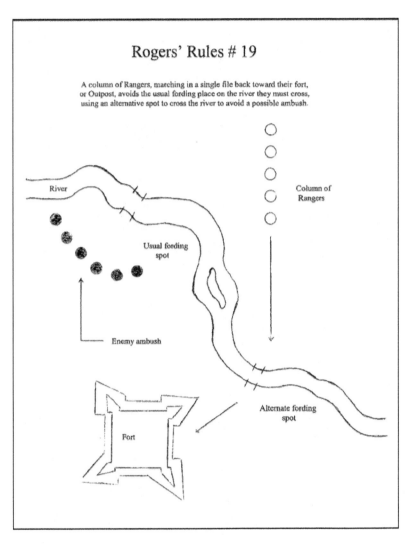

Rogers' Rules # 19

A column of Rangers, marching in a single file back toward their fort,
or Outpost, avoids the usual fording place on the river they must cross,
using an alternative spot to cross the river to avoid a possible ambush.

River

Column of
Rangers

Usual fording
spot

Enemy ambush

Alternate fording
spot

Fort

Figure 44.

Rogers' Rules:
Number Twenty

If you have to pass by lakes, keep at some distance from the edge of the water, lest, in case of an ambuscade or an attack from the enemy, when in that situation, your retreat should be cut off.

(Rogers, *Journals*, 61)

Rogers' Rule Number Nineteen instructed how to avoid being ambushed at the usual fording places along the rivers and streams that crisscrossed the Rangers' areas of operation during the French and Indian War. The Rangers faced many dangers during their scouts and missions around Lake George and Lake Champlain. Although the Rangers traveled on foot as well as by boat, sometimes they had to combine both methods of transportation. For example, they might move up the lake in whaleboats or canoes, then conceal the boats and continue their journey on land. Rogers warned his men in Rule Number Twenty to avoid marching too close to the water's edge, by which means the enemy might try to surround them and leave them no escape other than the water. As we have discussed before, many eighteenth-century soldiers could not swim, and even if they tried to escape by swimming out into the lake, their heavy clothing and gear could cause them to drown. In winter, the frigid temperature of the water could cause hypothermia, which could lead to death, even if the man did not drown. By marching at a distance from the edge of the water, Rogers and his Rangers ensured that they would have other openings or paths by which to force their way past the enemy. Then they could retreat until they found a piece of advantageous ground on which to make a stand or to scatter, each man taking a different route back to the appointed place of rendezvous. During a scout early in the war, some of Rogers' spies were discovered by the French, who tried to trap the Rangers between two fires at the edge of the water:

> I returned again towards the enemy, and the next evening sent two men to see if the enemy's centries were alert, who approached so near as to be discovered and fired at by them, and were so closely pursued in their retreat, that unhappily our whole party was discovered. The first notice I had of this being the case, was from two canoes with thirty men in them, which I concluded came out with the other party by land, in order to force us between two fires. (Rogers, *Journals*, 6)

The French tried to trap Rogers' party against the water's edge by sending the two canoes to stop their escape by water, and a party by land to surround them at the water's edge. Rogers however, went on the offensive by splitting his party, sending some out in their boats, which were fitted with wall-pieces, and attacked the two canoes. The remainder of his force he left on the shore to meet the advance of the French party marching towards them. After inflicting great damage on the enemy's canoes and wounding or killing several of the Indians inside them, Rogers returned to shore to pick up the rest of his party as they were coming under a brisk fire from the French land force. As the Rangers filed into the boats to make their escape, they again used their wall-pieces on the French forces on land, and forced them to retreat. Seeing the French force fleeing, the Rangers chased them back to their landing place in their boats, where 100 men reinforced the French. Rogers and his Rangers again discharged their wall-pieces at these new troops, but due to their superior numbers, they felt it was best to return to the British camp at Lake George.

The ability of the Rangers to go on the offensive, and the fact that they had boats outfitted with wall-pieces, enabled them to prevent the enemy from trapping them against the water's edge with no path of escape. Without the boats, they probably would have been surrounded and possibly wiped out, or at least have been forced to fight their way out of the ambush at considerable loss.

Another time that the Rangers were almost trapped by the water's edge, but were able to force their way past the enemy and escape in their concealed boats, was during a scout to draw a plan of the west end of Lake George and the enemy's works at Ticonderoga, in May of 1758:

> On the 30th, we proceeded down the lake in five whale-boats to the first narrows, and so on to the west end of the lake, where I took the plan his Lordship desired. Part of my party proceeded to reconnoiter Ticonderoga, and discovered a large encampment there, and a great number of Indians. While I was, with two or three others, taking a plan of the fort, encampment & c. I left the remainder of my party at some considerable distance; when I was returning to them, at the distance of 300 yards, they were fallen upon by a superior number of the enemy who had got between me and them. Capt. Jacobs, with the Mohegon Indians, run off at the first onset, calling to our people to run likewise; but they stood their ground, and discharged their pieces several times, at last broke through the enemy, by whom they were surrounded on all sides except their rear, where a river divided them: they killed three of the enemy, but lost eight of their own in this skirmish. My party rallied at the boats, where I joined them, and having collected all the slain together, we returned homewards. (Rogers, *Journals*, 99)

The ability to operate on land and water served the Rangers well on many occasions. The use of different kinds of vessels on the lakes and rivers allowed the Rangers to proceed by water, stop and conceal their boats, march overland to their objective, gain the needed intelligence or take prisoners, then march back to their boats and make a quick return by water. During the campaign to take the French stronghold at St. John, Rogers and his party worked in combination with two sloops under the command of Captain Grant. These vessels transported the Rangers' boats and provisions, as well as the Rangers themselves, to the place where they were to embark, and then kept cruising in the area in case the Rangers needed to escape in a hurry. After a battle at the French outpost at St. Therese, the Ranger force was pursued by a large body of French troops from Isle aux Noix. Rogers sent men ahead to make a prearranged signal to have the sloops come and pick them up, just as the enemy was approaching to try and trap them at the water's edge:

> I pursued my march with all possible speed: and the same day, being the 20th day of June, arrived at the lake opposite where the vessels lay; and as I sent a few men forward to repeat the signals, the boats met us at the shore. We directly put on board, the enemy soon appeared on the shore where we embarked. (Rogers, *Journals*, 169)

We can see the need to stay a proper distance from the edge of lakes and the larger rivers in order to prevent being trapped against the shoreline with no means to escape.

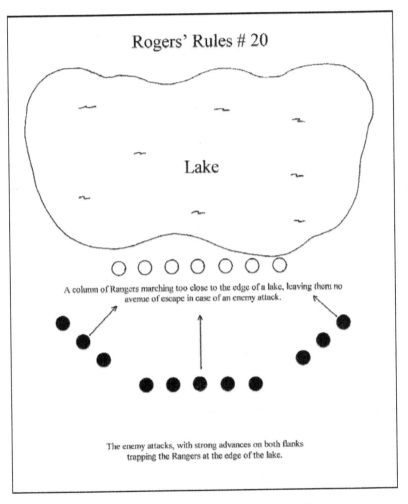

Figure 45. Trapped against the shore with no avenue of escape.

Rogers' Rules:
Number Twenty-One

If the enemy pursue your rear, take a circle till you come to your own tracks, and there form an ambush to receive them, and give them the first fire.

(Rogers, *Journals*, 61)

Rogers once again returned to the tried and true tactic of attacking the enemy from an ambush in Rule Number Twenty-One. Most soldiers, if they knew that the enemy was pursuing their track, would hasten their march back to the safety of their camp or post, but Rogers and his Rangers were not normal soldiers. Rogers wanted his men to go on the offensive—which we are learning was a Ranger trait—and circle around their own back-trail, setting an ambush for any of the enemy who might have discovered their tracks and were pursuing their party. A strong, alert rear guard, or the practice of sending men back to waylay the path the Rangers had come in on, informed the Rangers when they were being pursued. We have seen the effectiveness of a surprise attack on the enemy in our previous discussions. An ambush could be devastating on an enemy that was hot on the Rangers' trail like a pack of wolves, especially if in their excitement to catch their quarry they were not alert for an ambush.

An example of this method of ambushing an enemy coming from behind occurred during the General William Johnson's 1755 campaign against the French Fort St. Frederick at Crown Point.

The French had become aware of the British forces advancing against them from Lake George. They learned from their scouts and spies that there were only about 500 troops left to defend Fort Lydius (Edward). The French decided to attack that fort in its weakened condition, and then attack the British forces at Lake George.

Some British scouts found the trail of this large party of French troops on the march toward Fort Edward. General Johnson sent a mixed force of New England men and Indians, about 1000 men total, under the command of Colonel Williams and the Mohawk sachem Hendrick, or Teoniahigarawe. This force began its march to reinforce the men at Fort Edward.

Some of the French scouts brought in two prisoners who informed General Dieskau, the commander of the French force, that there was a large number of British troops marching on his back-trail. This information confirmed what the French had learned from two prisoners taken the day before near the British camp at Lake George. Dieskau, with his force of about 1500 men consisting of 600 Indians, 680 Canadians, and 220 Regular French troops, was caught between the 500 troops at Fort Edward and the 1000 British troops following his trail. Dieskau and his party could not attack the fort, for if the troops there were alerted to his plan to attack them, they could simply man the defenses of the fort until the 1000-man relief force reached them. The only answer was to try to attack the party marching towards him on his tracks.

General Dieskau used a variation of the tactic Rogers described in Rule Number 21; he prepared an ambush for the troops following him, by using his Canadians and Indians to attack the side of the British force, while his French Regulars met them head on:

> The report of the two prisoners induced M. de Dieskau to call a halt; he changed his order of march; the Canadians and Indians laid down their kit so to be lighter; he made them all pass to the left of the road, where they ambuscaded, in order not to be seen by the enemy, and to admit of the latter being engaged all at once. M. de Dieskau occupied the road with his troops. He had given orders that the Regulars should fire first, whereupon all the Canadians and Indians were to rush on the enemy. This arrangement

gave satisfaction to the Indians, because they had requested of M. de Dieskau the favor to allow them to attack the enemy in the woods, and he had always promised to grant them that privilege. (Hall, 80)

It has been said that some of the Indians with the French force warned the Indians with the British party of the ambush. Whatever the case, the trap was sprung prematurely, and the British forces, although with losses that included Colonel Williams, were able to conduct a fairly orderly retreat back towards the camp at Lake George. Hearing the sounds of the distant battle, General Johnson fortified the camp and was able to resist the French attack when it came. The British forces won the day, but if not for the failure of the Canadian and Indian ambush, the French may well have destroyed the relief party and then continued on to defeat the British at Lake George.

We can see the effectiveness of the tactic of circling around on your own track and setting up an ambush site against an enemy bent on catching your party. A scout led by Captain James Reed in November of 1755 almost fell under this type of trap. Captain Reed and a force of fifty men were sent out on a scout to discover what they could about the movements and disposition of the enemy, when they came upon a recently abandoned enemy campsite and began to pursue the tracks leading away from it:

28 Jest as the day Brock I went out with 4 men and trauiled 2 or 3 miles North Est and Came to a Camp which looked varey New and Judged to be made by the Enemy and we went in and thare fier was not all out But we Judged that they had begon 2 ouers or' more and they trauiled Right North and maid A Larg Road then I Returned to our Camp and sent out a Scout of 10 men which folowred that Road 3 miels and then thay Could not follow No further for the Enemy Scatrad and then thay could not tel which way they went and then thay Returned to the Camp our other Scouts mad no Descovery. (Hall, 49)

The scout followed this enemy party's tracks, but came to a point where the enemy had scattered, and the scouts could no longer follow their tracks. This party was lucky that the enemy force had not circled back on their tracks and laid an ambush for their pursuers.

The need for an alert rear guard, which would inform the party of their being pursued, as well as the tried and true tactic of the properly set ambush, could turn an enemy pursuit into a victory over one's foes. The ability to use a combination of Rogers' other rules, such as knowing the numbers of the pursuing party and deciding if an attack is likely to be a success, or if you should scatter your force to confuse your enemy as in the example set before, are hallmarks of the Rangers' ability to make split-second decisions; decisions that could save their lives.

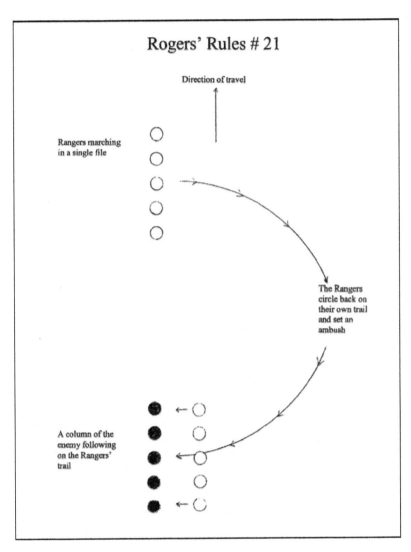

Figure 46. Circling back to set an ambush.

Rogers' Rules:
Number Twenty-Two

When you return from a scout, and come near our forts, avoid the usual roads, and avenues thereto, lest the enemy should have headed you, and lay in ambush to receive you, when almost exhausted with fatigues.

(Rogers, *Journals*, 62)

Just as Rogers warned in Rule Number Twenty-One against using the usual fords when crossing rivers and streams, here in Rule Number Twenty-Two he cautions against using the usual roads or paths leading back to the British forts. This was to avoid an enemy ambush, which would be likely on these well-used paths. The enemy, with their own spies and scouts, would be skulking around the forts and encampments, watching the British forces and trying to take prisoners or gain intelligence, just as the Rangers did.

The French and their Canadian and Indian allies were familiar with the commonly used roads leading to the forts and encampments, and would naturally try to ambush these busy thoroughfares. After Colonel Monro surrendered Fort William Henry in August of 1757, a party of Indians attacked the column of British, Provincial troops, and civilians that were marching along the road toward Fort Edward. These men were released under the terms of the surrender, and were to be allowed to return to Fort Edward, as long as they promised not to serve under arms for the British Army for the next eighteen months:

> The column at last got out of camp and began to move along the road that crossed the rough plain between the entrenchment and the forest, the Indians crowded upon them, impeded their march, snatched caps, coats, and weapons from men and officers, tomahawked those that resisted, and, seizing upon shrieking women and children, dragged them off or murdered them on the spot. It is said that some of the interpreters secretly fomented the disorder. Suddenly there rose the screech of the war-whoop. At this signal of butchery, which was given by Abenaki Christians from the mission of the Penobscot, a mob of savages rushed upon the New Hampshire men at the rear of the column, and killed or dragged away eighty of them. (Parkman, 296)

The French were particularly brutal in these attacks. Once they attacked a column of provisions on the road between Half-Way Brook and Fort Edward, scalping 110 people, and taking 84 prisoners:

> The second, likewise under the command of a Colonial Captain, which left the camp the latter part of July, fell in also on the Fort Edward road, at the enemy camp, with a convoy of 40 carts, each of which had from 4 to 6 oxen yoked to it; these carts were loaded with provisions, effects, merchandise, &ca. They destroyed them entirely. The oxen were killed; the carts burnt; the property pillaged by the Indians; 110 scalps were secured, and 84 prisoners taken; of these, 12 are women or girls. The escort, which was defeated, consisted of 40 men, commanded by a Lieutenant, who has been taken; the remainder of the men, who were killed or taken prisoners, consisted of wagoners, suttlers, traders, women and children. The English, 'tis known, feel this loss very sensibly. Some baggage and effects, belonging to General Abercrombie, as well as his music, were among the plunder. (Todish/Zaboly, 144)

The Rangers were well accustomed to the dangers of traveling along these roads between the forts and outposts of the Army. As we have discussed in earlier rules, the Rangers were often assigned as guards for the provision trains.

The Rangers were also adept ambushing the French along the roads and paths between the French posts. On a scout toward Crown Point in August of 1756, the Rangers set an ambush on the road leading to the fort:

> The 7th we lay in ambush by the road, with a design to intercept such as might come out to drive in the cattle; but no one appearing for that purpose, we approached nearer, to within half a mile of the fort, where we were discovered by two Frenchmen, before they were in our power. This accident obliged us to retreat, in which we killed upwards of forty cattle. We arrived at Fort William-Henry, August 10. (Rogers, *Journals*, 23)

The Rangers used this way of ambushing the usual roads to effect a total surprise of the garrison at the French Fort St. Therese. The Rangers had been assigned to go and attack the French at St. Johns, but finding it too well guarded, they went on and reconnoitered the French at St. Therese, located about three miles from St. Johns:

> I observed two large store-houses in the inside, and that the enemy were carting hay into the fort. I waited for an opportunity when the cart had just entered the gate-way, run forward, and got into the fort before they could clear the way for shutting the gate. I had at this time sent different parties to the several houses, about fifteen in number, which were near the fort, and were all surprised at the same instant of time, and without firing a single gun. We took in the fort twenty-four soldiers, and in the houses seventy-eight prisoners, women and children included. (Rogers, *Journals*, 168)

By laying in wait along the road leading to the fort, the Rangers were able to spring their trap at such a time as to allow them to capture the fort without firing a shot. Rogers was also smart enough to spring his trap on the houses that were built near the fort. If Rogers had not addressed the inhabitants, they could have mounted an attack on the Ranger force from these houses.

Another thing that Rogers cautioned against in this rule was the fact that the Rangers returning from their scout may have been exhausted, and not as alert as they should be. It would be common for something like this to happen: The Rangers have just returned from a long scout, deep into enemy territory, where death could be behind any tree. They would be happy to be almost home, and would possibly be tired and hungry. It would be easy to drop their guard at this time and fall victim to an ambush. The rigors of the type of scouts the Rangers conducted may be hard to fathom, but Rogers' journals are full of references to Rangers being sent back from a scout early because they were tired or sick:

> On the 18th in the morning, eight of my party being tired, returned to the fort; with the remainder I marched nine miles further. (Rogers, *Journals*, 65)

The snow was about three inches deep when the Rangers began this scout, and by the next morning, after camping for the night, it had increased to about fifteen inches deep, which would have made for more difficult and fatiguing travel. Rogers once stopped and hunted for meat before making the rest of the way back from a scout:

> We found our boat in safety, and had the good fortune (after being almost exhausted with hunger, cold, and fatigue) to kill two deer, with which being refreshed, on the 24th we returned to Fort William-Henry. (Rogers, *Journals*, 9)

This shows the importance of being well rested and fed before returning to their forts, so that the Rangers could be at their most alert when almost home.

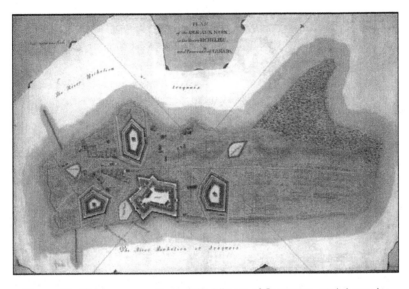

Figure 47. This map, courtesy of the Library of Congress, and drawn by Captain Thomas Walker of the 60th Royal American Regiment, shows the French fortifications on Isle aux Noix in the Richelieu River. In 1760, Robert Rogers, commanding a force of 275 Rangers and 25 Light Infantry men, was ordered by General Amherst to try to surprise the garrison on Isle aux Noix, and after capturing the fort, to proceed to the French Fort Chambly. The garrison at Isle aux Noix was alert, and Rogers felt that there was not any hope of a surprise attack, so he and his command instead targeted Fort St. Therese, which they took without firing a shot. The French Army under the command of General Levis was besieging the British Forces in command of Quebec. This thrust by Rogers was an attempt by General Amherst to force the French to lift the siege, and contend with the British forces making their way toward Canada by the water/land route along the Richelieu River. These actions, as well as others Rogers and his Rangers participated in during the 1760 campaigns, were successful in causing the French to pull some of their soldiers from the siege lines around Quebec, and send them to confront these attacks on the French forts along the river.

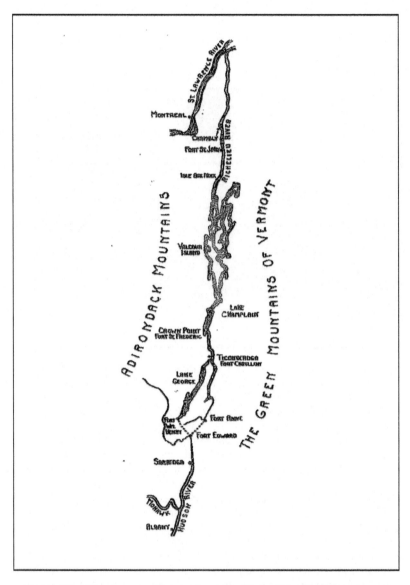

Figure 48. This map, courtesy of the collections of the Fort Ticonderoga Museum, shows the locations of the French fortifications at Chambly, St. Jean, (John) and Isle aux Noix, in relation to Forts Ticonderoga and Crown Point. These forts guarded the passageway into Canada, by way of the Richelieu River. Special thanks to museum curator Christopher Fox for his aid in the use of this map.

Rogers' Rules:
Number Twenty-Three

When you pursue any party that has been near our forts or encampments, follow not directly in their tracks, lest they should be discovered by their rear-guards, who, at such a time, would be most alert; but endeavour, by a different route, to head them and met them in some narrow pass, or lay in ambush to receive them when and where they least expect it.

(Rogers, *Journals*, 62)

This rule is another example of the way that Rogers always tried to think ahead and use absolutely any tactic available to gain an advantage over the enemy. In Rule Number Twenty-One, Rogers cautioned the Rangers about the enemy following on their back-trail, and instructed them to circle back and set an ambush. In Rule Number Twenty-Three, Rogers issued the same advice, this time applying it to when the Rangers were pursuing a party of the enemy who were returning to their forts or outposts after scouting the British forts or encampments. Rogers warned not to follow directly on the tracks of the fleeing enemy party, but instead to try to get ahead of the enemy and set the highly effective ambush. This was especially important, because after raiding into British territory, the enemy's rear guard would be expecting pursuit and would be at their highest level of alertness. Just as Rogers advised the Rangers in Rule Number Twenty-One, the enemy could circle back on their trail and ambush the pursuing party. By trying to get ahead of the fleeing enemy, the Rangers could avoid the problem of falling into a possible ambush. Evidently, this was something that the Rangers did on occasion, as a reference to a Ranger scout in the papers of Colonel Gage attests:

> To Head or cut off any party of the Enemy, that may come out by way of Wood creek, South, or East Bay, (if discovered seasonably) 'Twould be advisable to go down the Lake in Boats, & cross over the Mountains to the Narrows North of South Bay & Lay there in Ambush for them against their return. (Todish/Zaboly, 129, 130)

It may seem impossible to get ahead of your enemy after a raid, but if the enemy party has taken any prisoners, their retreat may be slow. The Rangers were very familiar with their areas of operation, and knew of many routes that could allow them to get ahead of the enemy.

Once, after attacking a convoy of ox carts, the French were returning toward home with 84 prisoners, many of them women and children, which definitely would have slowed their retreat:

> Captain Henry Champion records this incident in his journal on July 27: "This day was killed and missing 25 men between Fort Edward and halfway brook, one lieutenant-Stephens, one teamsman, one Sargt. -Wells of Windsor, ye regt. provost and 30 women and children, 38 teams and wagons destroyed with their carts and loading." (Todish/Zaboly, 130)

Some of the people attacked on this provision train were able to flee and escape their captors. They ran back towards the safety of Fort Edward or tried to hide in the woods. These survivors soon spread the word of the attack and of the enemy's retreat with their prisoners in tow:

> A few terror-stricken fugitives found their way back to Fort Edward. A relief party was formed and the alarm cannon boomed. When it was heard at the Halfway Brook post, part of the garrison marched out and fell in with the rear of the foe which had become intoxicated with the liquor taken as

plunder. But the provincials refused to attack. Abercromby got the news by nine o'clock in the evening. Major Rogers and Major Putnam were ordered to assemble seven hundred men for the pursuit. The anxious General stayed up to two o'clock in the morning to see them off. Later he dispatched one thousand men under Colonel Haviland with orders to support Rogers. Then he nervously awaited news of the result. On 30 July a message came in from Haviland, the enemy had been far down the lake when Rogers came up. (Cuneo, 88, 89)

The enemy was particularly brutal in this attack, even going to the trouble to scalp one of the oxen in the provision train.

There is a unique sidelight to this engagement. Scalping was a fairly common practice by both sides, but it took an interesting twist here. Captain-Lieutenant Henry Skinner of the Royal Artillery makes the following comment in his Journal on July 17, 1759, nearly a year later: "The commanding Officer of this party [Pierre {or Louis} St. Luc de la Corne] is the man who butchered our bullock escort last campaign; at which affair they were so wanton in their barbarities, that they scalped an ox." (Todish/Zaboly, 130)

The enemy had a big head start on the force under Rogers and Putnam, who tried their hardest to catch them. Both Putnam and Rogers had been on many scouts towards the French forts and encampments, and would have been able to make "educated guesses" as to the most likely route the French raiders would take to get back home with their prisoners. This could possibly enable the pursuing party to take a different route than the enemy, and get ahead of them. Rogers himself implies that this might have been the plan in one of his journal entries:

In pursuit of this party, with a design to intercept their retreat, I was ordered to embark the 18th with 700 men; the enemy however escaped me. (Rogers, *Journals*, 106)

By saying that the plan was to intercept the enemy's retreat, we can assume that Rogers was going to try to take a different route to the path the enemy was going to use in their retreat, and try to get there first. The Rangers and the rest of the British force were not able to catch the enemy party, but evidently were right on their heels. One of Major Rogers' sergeants described the scene:

> "Said Sargt. Says they saw ye party of enemy going down South Bay that did ye mischief the 28th, said party about 300; they saw three women alive in one bateau, but our men were about half an hour too late to give them fire." (Todish/Zaboly, 134)

The French party had several hours' head start on the Rangers and the mixed force that pursued them under Rogers and Putnam. Even with such a head start, the Rangers were able to get close enough to the retreating raiders to see some of the prisoners in their bateaux as the party started back up the lake toward home. This is another tribute to the Rangers and their ability to react quickly and be able to march at a minute's warning. Rogers also knew that in order to secure the release of some of the prisoners, the pursuit had to be lightning quick, to prevent the French force from separating into smaller parties so their escape would be easier. The use of the ambush, in which the enemy was hit by total surprise, gave the Rangers the best chance of confusing the enemy and allowing the prisoners to be rescued before the French could kill them and escape into the forest or up the lake.

Rogers' Rules: Number Twenty-Four

If you are to embark in canoes, battoes, or otherwise, chuse the evening for the time of your embarkation, as you will then have the whole night before you, to pass undiscovered by any parties of the enemy, on hills, or other places, which command a prospect of the lake or river you are upon.

(Rogers, *Journals*, 62)

Robert Rogers and his Rangers have been called the "Falcons of the Lakes." They swooped down upon their enemies quickly and accurately like a bird to its prey. The areas of their major conflicts were the lakes and rivers from Canada to Albany, New York, as well as the military sites from the Richelieu River to Lakes Champlain and George, down the Hudson and Mohawk Rivers. The St. Lawrence River, as well as Lakes Huron, Michigan, Erie and Ontario all played major parts in the French and Indian War. The rivers and lakes were the young nation's highways, and the vessels that plied her waters were yesterday's automobiles. Nearly all of the major military operations of the time involved some form of lake or river transportation, as well as support from the navy. The types of vessels used ranged from the smallest bark canoes to British or French men of war.

Pursuant to orders from Major-General Johnson, Commander in chief of the Provincial Forces, raised for the reduction of Crown-Point, I embarked with four men upon Lake George, to reconnoiter the strength of the enemy, and proceeding down the lake twenty-five miles, I landed on the west side, leaving two men in charge of the boat... (Rogers, *Journals*, 1)

This is the very first journal entry of Major Robert Rogers' exploits in the French and Indian War. Rogers did not identify the type of boat he used during this mission, but water travel clearly had its advantages. Although they risked being seen from land, Rogers and his men were able to travel twenty-five miles in one day. Covering that distance would have taken much longer over the rugged terrain and through the thick forests in the area. Both the French and the English realized the importance of the waterways in a military situation:

On October 15, 1730, Beauharnois sent a letter to the king of France with a recommendation to build a fort at Crown Point on Lake Champlain. Beauharnois suggested that, "When in possession of Crown Point the road will be blocked on the English should they wish to pass over our territory." (Bellico, 17)

By road, Beauharnois means the water route up or down Lake Champlain. This corresponds to the direction of water flow on a body of water, not the direction up or down, or to a point on a compass. This shows the importance of the area waterways, and the need to protect them:

October 7, 1775, I received orders of this date from General Johnson, to reconnoiter the French troops at Ticonderoga. Accordingly, I proceeded at night to a point of land on the west side of the lake, where we landed, hid our canoe, and left two men in charge of it. The next day, with the other three, I marched to the Point at Ticonderoga, where we arrived about noon. (Rogers, *Journals*, 3)

We know that on this excursion, the vessel was a canoe. Rogers traveled at night to reduce the possibility of being seen. He proceeded to a point away from his destination, and then marched overland to Ticonderoga. Rogers used a combination of water and land routes on this scout, as we have discussed in some of his earlier rules. This tactic also prevented the enemy from using the hills and mountains to their advantage while spying on the British forces using the waterways:

> Having made what discoveries we could, we began our return, in which we found that the enemy had a large advanced guard at the north end of Lake George, where it issues out of it into Lake Champlain. While we were there, I perceived a bark canoe, with nine Indians and a Frenchman in it, going up the lake. (Rogers, *Journals*, 3)

This entry provides information about the canoes that were used in the area. Rogers specifically described a bark canoe. The trader, Alexander Henry, gives us an example of a bark canoe:

> Next morning at ten o'clock we reached the shore of Lake Ontario. Here we are employed two days in making canoes out of the bark of the elm tree in which we were to transport ourselves to Niagara. For this purpose, the Indians first cut a tree, then stripped off the bark in one entire sheet of about eighteen feet in length, the incision being lengthwise. The canoe was now complete as to its top, bottom and sides. The ends were next closed by sewing the bark together, and a few ribs and bars being introduced, the architecture was finished. In this manner, we made two canoes, of which one carried eight men and the other nine. (Henry, 111, 112)

Henry described the construction method and the size of the canoes his party used in the Great Lakes region. The real surprise is that they were not made of the well-known birch bark, but of elm:

> "In late September Reverend John Cleaveland, with the Massachusetts provincial soldiers provided a rare delineation of the construction of Indian canoes in his journal. After dinner one evening, he walked down to the shore of Lake George to view two captured birch bark canoes, the largest of which was thirty-five feet in length, five feet wide, and designed to carry twenty men. The inside was made "with cedar clap boards thin as brown paper and

laid lengthwise of ye canoe upon which crossways of ye canoe is another laying of cedar." (Bellico, 74-75)

Figure 49. A reproduction birch bark canoe manned by modern Ranger reenactors. This photograph was taken at the Grand Encampment #2 at Stony Creek Metro Park in Michigan.

From what we have learned, the canoe would seem to be a very efficient, fast and easily made form of watercraft, but further investigation leads us to see otherwise:

The last of these arguments was with me so powerful that though a bark canoe was a vehicle to which I was altogether a stranger, though this was a very small one of only sixteen or eighteen feet in length and very much out of repair, and though the misfortune which I had experienced in the navigation of these rocky parts of the St. Lawrence when descending with the army naturally presented itself to my mind as a still further discouragement, yet I was not long in resolving to undertake the voyage. Accordingly, after stopping the leaks as completely as we were able, we embarked and proceeded. My fears were not lessened by perceiving that the least unskillful motion was sufficient to overset the ticklish craft into which I had ventured; by the reflection that a shock comparatively gently from a mass of rock or ice was more that its frail material could sustain... nor by observing that the ice, which lined the shores of the river, was too strong to be pushed through and at the same time too weak to be walked upon, so that in the event of disaster it would be almost impossible to reach the land. In fact, we had not proceeded more than a mile when our canoe became full of water, and it was not till after a long search that we found a place of safety. (Henry, 4)

Canoes were very easy to carry overland if necessary, and they could be operated in very shallow rivers and streams due to their light construction, but we also know that while they were fast and easy to build, they were tricky to use and were very fragile, requiring frequent repair:

The small roots of the spruce tree afford the wattap, with which the bark is sewed; and the gum of the pine tree supplies the place of tar and oakum. Bark, some spare wattap, and gum are always carried in each canoe for the repairs which frequently become necessary. (Henry, 7)

Evidence shows us that Robert Rogers and his Rangers used canoes many times, in certain circumstances. We also know that canoes would not serve in all instances and required a lot of maintenance:

November 4, 1755 Agreeable to orders from General Johnson this day, I embarked for the enemies advanced guard before mentioned, with a party of thirty men in four battoes, mounted with two wall pieces each. (Rogers, *Journals*, 5)

Rogers mentioned a different type of watercraft in this journal entry, the bateau:

Bateaux were common on Lake George during the French and Indian War. They were pointed at bow and stern, made of pine and oak wood. They could be rowed or poled in shallow water, and had an oar off the stern for steering. (Starbuck, 187)

Bateaux were usually outfitted with a single mast and sail. Rogers mentioned them many times, on missions consisting of small as well as large numbers of men. The larger boats would have been more stable on the lakes and larger rivers, and the sail would have made for quick travel when blessed by favorable winds. This leads us to believe that the Rangers would have needed a basic knowledge of sailing and the associated rigging that even a boat of this size would have required. This argument is furthered by the following quote.

Ranger Captain Tute's method of rigging blanket sails (which had been used earlier) was adopted, with each bateau rigged with two blankets. (Bellico, 98)

Figure 50. A reproduction troop landing craft, filled with British Regulars, also taken at Stony Creek Metro Park in Michigan at the 2004 Grand Encampment.

This quote shows the resourcefulness of the Rangers in learning to adapt in a situation of which some of them may not have been accustomed. It also shows that some of the Rangers may have been acquainted with boats before the war. Knowing the basics of rigging a sail, which would involve a system of ropes and knots, and improvising by using a blanket in place of a sail, shows how adaptable the Rangers really were. By utilizing the blankets as makeshift sails, the Rangers were able to outrun the pursuing French boats and effectively make their escape.

The boats of the day were another useful tool for the Rangers, just as important as their muskets and other gear. The Rangers' use of boats went hand in hand with the tactical use of the quick hit-and-run raid. The waterways allowed the Rangers to travel to and escape from the enemy much more quickly than if they made the entire scout on foot.

Rogers' Rules:
Number Twenty-Five

In paddling or rowing, give orders that the boat or canoe next the sternmost, wait for her, and the third for the second, and the fourth for the third, and so on, to prevent separation, and that you may be ready to assist each other on any of emergency.

(Rogers, *Journals*, 62)

With the possibility of rough water or storms, this rule was absolutely necessary for the safety of the Rangers when they traveled by water. This tactic saved the lives of a crew on Lake Ontario during the trip to accept the surrender of the western French forts and outposts in late 1760:

> The boats in a line. If the wind rose high, the red flag hoisted, and the boats to croud nearer, that they may be ready to give mutual assistance in case of a leak or other accident; by which means we saved the crew and arms of the boat commanded by Lieutenant M'Cormack, which sprung a leak and sunk, losing nothing except their packs. (Rogers, *Journals*, 189)

The number of boats used during the military campaigns of the French and Indian War sometimes was considerable:

The colonies fell down on their quotas and fewer than ten thousand men were on hand July 4, 1758, when the combined army of sixteen thousand took to the water and rowed down the lake. Nine hundred bateaux, one hundred and thirty five whaleboats, and rafts of artillery covered the width of the lake and extended several miles, as colorful a military spectacle as the war had seen. (Peckham, 166)

What a convoy this must have been! Bateaux must have been the mainstay of the British Army, as 900 of them set out against Ticonderoga. The safety measures taken for such a large convoy of boats was very important:

It is recommended to the soldiers as well as officers, not to mind the waves of the Lake; but when the surf is high to stick to their oars, and the men at the helm to keep the boat quartering on the waves, and briskly follow, then no mischief will happen by any storm whatever. Ten of the best steersmen amongst the Rangers are to attend Captain Campbell and company in his boats. It is likewise recommended to the officers commanding in those boats, to hearken to the steersmen in a storm or bad weather, in managing their boats. At evening, (if it is thought necessary to row in the night time) a blue flag will be hoisted in the Major's boat, which is the signal for the boats to dress, and then proceed in the following manner: the boats next to the hindermost, are to wait for the two in the rear, the two third boats for the second two; and so on to the boats leading a-head, to prevent separation, which in the night would be hazardous. (Todish/Zaboly, 214)

The boats must have been very strong and well built to put the lives of so many in their trust. The bateau appears to have been the workhorse of the day, well suited for the task at hand. This strength allowed them to serve many different purposes in many different ways:

The pontoon arrangement of bateau with the artillery was finally brought into the small cove on the southwest shore of the lake after nightfall. Twelve cannon and a few mortars were unloaded. (Bellico, 47)

The method mentioned above usually meant three bateaux were lashed together, with a platform built on top of them for transporting artillery. When we think of the weight of colonial era cannon and mortars, even small ones, the strength of the bateau is clearly evident:

> The floating batteries and rafts were hastily constructed at Lake George while most of the bateaux were built in Albany and Schenectady under Colonel John Bradstreet, commander of the battoe service. (Bellico, 60)

Colonel John "Jean Baptiste" Bradstreet was an American-born Regular officer. He was in charge of the men who manned the bateaux for the British Army. He even took temporary charge of the retreating army after its defeat at Ticonderoga in 1758. Colonel Bradstreet was well known for using his bateau men in cooperation with the army to great advantage. For the British Army to place a colonel in charge of this service shows how vital it was to the Crown.

Would the workhorse of the British Army serve all of the needs of the Rangers, or would a happy medium between the bateau and the canoe be needed?

It is believed that the new commander in chief after the death of General Braddock, William Shirley, gave some whaleboats to Robert Rogers for use by his Rangers. Rogers himself proves this with the following journal entry:

> About this time the General augmented my company to seventy men and sent me six light whaleboats from Albany, with orders to proceed immediately to Lake Champlain, to cut off if possible, the provisions and flying parties of the enemy accordingly. (Rogers, *Journals*, 18)

Rogers implied that the whaleboats were a lighter, faster craft than the bateaux that they had been using. A lighter and faster boat would have been better suited to the quick strike methods of the Rangers:

> Double ended round bottomed boat used for whaling. In the military this type of boat was used to carry primarily light troops because of its quickness compared to a bateau. (Kemmer, 160)

Lighter weight combined with speed in a strong, more easily manned boat, made it perfect for use by Rangers or light infantry. A boat that was fast enough to chase down whales must have been very sleek, and cut through the water with ease:

> Amherst described the whaleboats in 1759 as being "28 feet in the keel, 5 feet and 2 inches broad, 25 inches deep, 34 feet from stem to stern...with seven oars besides the steering oar." (Bellico, 90)

We can see another way that the British Army was beginning to understand and adapt to warfare in the New World. While the bateau was the workhorse of the day, the whaleboat would have been the thoroughbred. These lighter boats benefited the Rangers, because carrying the heavy bateaux across land was very difficult:

> The difficulties of portaging are attested by the fact that it took four days to cover about four miles on an airline. (Cuneo, 36)

Portaging meant carrying the boats around dangerous water obstacles such as rapids or waterfalls. A good example is the "Great Portage" around the Niagara Falls.

The Rangers frequently used portaging to gain a tactical advantage over their enemy:

> In early October, the French found four whaleboats abandoned in a little cove on the eastern shore above Crown Point, one "mounted with three swivels." Rogers, following a scouting expedition to St. Jean on the Richelieu River in late August had hid the whaleboats. The vessels had been laboriously carried over on the east side of Lake George near present day Huletts Landing to Lake Champlain. (Bellico, 38, 39)

This was a source of great concern for the French. They could not imagine how the British Army could have found a water route that they were unaware of. Portaging whaleboats over rough, hilly terrain, under combat conditions would test anyone's endurance. I am sure the Rangers were glad that they were transporting the lighter, sleeker whaleboats, rather than the heavier bateaux.

Rogers himself tells of another unique way in which his whaleboats were transported to a place of need:

> His Lordship immediately ordered me out with fifty men in whaleboats, which were carried over in wagons to Lake George. (Rogers, *Journals*, 98)

Boats normally were carried around portage areas by sheer strength and numbers of men. One last quote shows the frequency with which the whaleboats were carried from place to place, enabling them to be put into action at a moment's notice:

> For completion of this order I had sixty Rangers in one English flat bottomed boat and two whaleboats, in which, after night came on I embarked and passed over to the other side of Lake Champlain. (Rogers, *Journals*, 128)

An explanation of the entry by Rogers is as follows:

> These boats were carried across the land from Lake George to Lake Champlain. (Rogers, *Journals*, 128)

Not only was the British Army adapting, but so were Rogers and his Rangers. As their skill and daring increased, so did their willingness to try for bigger prizes.

Part of Great Britain's problem stemming from the three earlier conflicts that led to the final French and Indian War, was the fact that the people and the government were against maintaining a large standing army. As Spain began to lose its standing in the world order, Britain had become the world's major naval power. Britain's conquests were won by its naval strength, not by having thousands of troops at its disposal. It is only natural that the Rangers had contact with some of the larger vessels of both the French and British navies:

> There had been signs of the enemy from the first opening of spring. In the intervals of fog, rain, and snow squalls, sails were seen hovering on the distant sea, and during the latter part of May a squadron of nine ships cruised off the mouth of the harbor, appearing and disappearing, sometimes driven away by gales, sometimes lost in fogs, and sometimes approaching to within cannon shot of the batteries. Their object was to blockade the port, in which

they failed, for French ships had come in at intervals, till as we have seen, twelve of them lay safe anchored in the harbor, with more than a years provisions for the garrison. At length on the first of June, the southeastern horizon was white with a cloud of canvas. (Parkman, 336)

Here we are treated to a vivid detail of the actions of the British and French navies. Think of the horizon awash in a display of canvas, the gun ports lining the sides of the might of the British Navy. We can almost see the sailors climbing the rigging, bringing the ships to life. In the next quote, we are introduced to some ship designations and purposes:

At the end of May, Admiral Boscawen was at Halifax with twenty three ships of the line, eighteen frigates, and fire ships, and a fleet of transports, on board of which were eleven thousand and six hundred soldiers, all regulars, except 500 provincial rangers. (Parkman, 336)

Ships of the line are British men of war, or heavily armed warships that cannot only do battle at sea, but can also bombard land emplacements. Twenty-three of them must have been an impressive sight to the Rangers aboard the transports, especially those from the frontier who might never have seen a ship of that size. Major Rogers came across many smaller armed warships in his battles on the lakes and rivers:

This day being July 7th, 30 boats and a schooner of about 30 or forty tons passed by us towards Canada. (Rogers, *Journals*, 19)

The purpose of many of these vessels was to transport furs and other goods. They were now being used to help the war effort:

A contemporary newspaper described the "Earl of Halifax", 51 feet keel, and about 100 tons burthen ... to carry 18 6 and 4 pounders, 20 swivels, 50 sailors and a company of Marines. (Bellico, 74)

Rogers and his Rangers, over the course of the French and Indian War, were responsible for the capture of many larger French ships. The Rangers as well as the British Army knew that the waterways must be cleared of the French Navy before the army could progress against the enemy on land:

> In one action in July Rogers reported pursuing two vessels, "lighters or shallops" (probably small sailing galleys), which were sunk with their cargoes near Button Bay on Lake Champlain. (Bellico, 38)

Rogers himself attests to the capture of larger vessels with the following description:

> I soon got opposite the vessels, and by firing from the shore, gave an opportunity to some of my party to swim on board with their tomahawks, and took one of the vessels, in the meantime Col. Darby had got on board the Radeau and had her manned. (Rogers, *Journals*, 163)

A radeau was essentially a floating battery, well suited for use on the lakes against the French forts and encampments. These floating batteries, as well as many of the other boats used in eighteenth-century military campaigns, were built on site, and then launched upon the lakes and streams in the areas that they were needed. Many of the soldiers of the British Army must have had some experience in shipbuilding, from the numbers of boats that were used during the war:

> "Radeau," meaning raft in French, denoted the flat-bottomed nature of the ship. The lower sides of a Radeau inclined slightly outward while the upper sides or bulwarks curved inward at a steep angle over the interior of the vessel. The upper sides were "planked up higher than a mans head shelving in or arching inwards to defend ye men's bodies and heads, with port-holes for ye cannon" and contrived so that tis impossible for the enemy to board her." The Radeau was equipped with a large number of sweeps (oars) with a design for one or two masts and square sails. (Bellico, 75)

A quote from the journals of 2nd Lt. Thomas Moody gives us a glimpse of the action aboard a radeau:

> This morning a very unfortunate accident. One of the ruddos was ordered to cover the grenigers who went to land

one (sic) the point opposite to the fort. A shot which was the second that was sent from the enemy Capt. Legg of the Royal Artillery both his leggs shot off died soon after. Christopher Langley the calf of his leg shot away. Nathaniel March both of his legs. James Urin of our company shot off by the knee. The amputation was above. Robert Towerson the top of his knee which was amputated. This morn I was ordered with 60 men of our rigiment to carry provisions down to a small island where I had view of the poor unhappy persons above mentioned. We hear that it was 6 that was wounded in the manner following: the rodo went very near the fort and fired several times without any return. Then they tacked about on which the French fired. The men sitting on the quarter deck which raked them in the manner following manner (sic). The ball went forward and lodged in the knave of a wheel. Returned from the island about 12 clock. (Moody 26)

Imagine the smoke and the noise of the guns, the screaming of the wounded and the dying. The debris on the deck, tangled with the men and the rigging.

An original radeau from the French and Indian War is sunk in near perfect condition in Lake George. After being sunk to protect it during the winter months, the radeau was never raised the following spring. Named the *Land Tortoise*, it is protected in a New York State Submerged Heritage Preserve, which preserves this important window to our past.

Some of the other boats that plied the waters of Lake George and Lake Champlain were called brigs, which were large, well-armed vessels.

"On August 29, the Brigantine ... will mount twenty guns," but other reports noted "six 6 pounders, twelve four pounders, and twenty swivels." (Bellico, 98)

At 155 tons, this was probably one of the largest ships to grace the lakes during the French and Indian War. We are also told of a strange way that the British Army protected the all-important naval ships in wintertime, in the following quote from Bellico:

The sloop *Halifax, Land Tortoise*, row galleys, and other vessels at the lake, including 260 bateaux, were sunk in the depths of Lake George for protection. Because Fort William Henry had been destroyed by the French during the summer of 1757, the ships could not be safeguarded at a garrisoned fort over the winter. Leaving the vessels exposed would certainly result in their destruction, as had occurred during a French raid across the ice in March 1757. Placing them in cold storage at the bottom of the lake with retrieval planned for the spring of 1759 was the only option available. (Bellico, 75, 76)

To go to such trouble to sink and then raise that number of ships shows the importance of the vessels and the importance of protecting them for the campaigns ahead.

The ships were sunk by filling the hulls with rocks, or "ballast stones," which were unloaded the next spring to allow the boats to float to the surface. This also kept the wood of which the boats were made swollen with water. If the wooden boats had been allowed to dry out, they would have leaked very badly, and been of no use to the army.

Rogers' Rules:
Number Twenty-Six

Appoint one man in each boat to look out for fires, on
the adjacent shores, from the numbers and size of which
you may be able to form some judgment of the number
that kindled them, and whether you are able to attack
them or not.

(Rogers, *Journals*, 63)

This rule is just another way that Rogers instructed his Rangers
to be alert at all times, to take notice of their surroundings, and
to constantly gather information based on their observations.

As the Rangers passed the shorelines bordering the lakes and
streams they traveled upon, Rogers cautioned them to keep a
lookout for the enemy's campfires, which would reveal the
location of their encampments. To pass by a section of land or an
island that held a number of the enemy without noticing their
presence, would be to invite disaster on the scouting mission. An
undetected enemy party would be in the way of the Rangers'
retreat if the Rangers were discovered and forced to return home.
This enemy party could trap the Rangers between themselves and
a pursuing party.

This tactic of putting one man in each boat to look out for the
fires of the enemy was employed many times during the course of

the Rangers' operations along the Lake George and Champlain corridor:

> In this manner we proceeded, till dusk, down Lake George to Sabbath Day Point, where the army halted and refreshed. About ten o'clock the army moved again, when my Lord How went in front with his whale-boat, Lieutenant Col. Broadstreet's and mine, with Lieutenant Holmes, in another, whom he sent forward to go near the landing place, and observe if the enemy was posted there. Holmes returned about day-break, met the army near the Blue Mountains, within four miles of the landing - place, and reported that there was a party of the enemy at the landing place, which he discovered by their fires. (Rogers, *Journals*, 101)

These fires turned out to be the encampment of the French advanced guard. This action was part of the 1758 advance of the British Army up Lake George towards the French at Ticonderoga. The French had their scouts and spies watching the advance of the army up the lake. This information, of the location of the enemy at the British Army's intended landing place was critical for the disposition of the troops, and the success of the landing parties. The presence of, and numbers of the fires seen could help the Rangers to make a fairly accurate estimate as to the number of the enemy in the encampment.

On June 28, 1756, the Rangers were sent on a scout towards the French encampments at Ticonderoga and Crown Point. As the Rangers passed silently by the French at Ticonderoga, they were able to estimate the number of troops there:

> We embarked then again, and passed by Ticonderoga undiscovered, tho' we were so near the enemy as to hear their centry's watch-word. We judged from the number of their fires, that they had a body of about 2000 men, and the lake at this place to be near 400 yards wide. (Rogers, *Journals*, 18, 19)

This is another tribute to the Rangers and some of the daring scouting missions that they undertook during the course of the war. This scout consisted of fifty men, but the Rangers were still willing to pass what could be an enemy force as large as 2000 men, and still go on towards Crown Point to gain the critical information that was so needed by the British Army.

Sometimes, what appeared to be the fires of the enemy, might be found out to be something else altogether. This occurred during a scout in which the Rangers traveled over the frozen lake on ice skates. One of the Rangers thought he saw a fire on an adjacent shore. The Rangers were once again traveling at night to help hide their movements:

> We halted at a place called Sabbath-day Point, on the west side of the lake, and sent our parties to look down the lake with perspective glasses, which we had for that purpose. As soon as it was dark we proceeded down the lake. I sent Lieutenant Phillips with fifteen men, as an advanced guard, some of whom went before him on skates, While Ensign Rofs flanked us on the left under the west-shore, near which we kept the main body, marching as close as possible, to prevent separation, it being a very dark night. In this manner we continued our march within eight miles of the shore, French advanced guards, When Lieutenant Phillips sent a man on skates back to me, to desire me to halt; upon which I ordered my men to squat down on the ice. Mr. Phillips soon came to me himself, leaving his party to look out, and said, he imagined he had discovered a fire on the east-shore, but was not certain; upon which I sent him with Ensign White to make further discovery. In about an hour they returned, fully persuaded that a party of the enemy was encamped there. I then called in the advanced guard, and flanking party, and marched on to the west-shore, where, in a thicket, we hid our sleys and packs, leaving a small guard with them, and with the remainder I marched to attack the enemy's encampment, if there was any; but when we came near the place, no fires were to be seen, which made us conclude that we had mistaken some bleach patches of snow, or pieces of rotten wood, for fire (which in the night, at a distance resembles it) where-upon we returned to our packs, and there lay the remainder of the night without fire. (Rogers, *Journals*, 74, 75)

It was later learned that indeed, a party of the enemy had been encamped there, but they had discovered Rogers' advanced party, put out their fire, and retreated to Ticonderoga to warn of the Rangers' approach.

We can see how important the knowledge of the presence of the enemy was. This scout led to the worst defeat that the Rangers would suffer during the French and Indian War. The French party sounded the alarm that the Rangers were in the area, and the French were on their guard, which led to the engagement known as the "Second Battle on Snowshoes." If the Rangers had known that the French party had been at the encampment and had become aware of the Rangers' presence, they could have returned to their home base, or altered their course or objectives, and saved many lives. As it was, by assuming that some snow or rotten wood had been mistaken for the fires of the enemy, the Rangers proceeded on their mission, and a date with disaster. If the Rangers had discovered the remnants of the French fires, they could have made the determination to follow this party, and possibly attack them, or if the party was too large, to retreat in the face of superior numbers.

Rogers' Rules:
Number Twenty-Seven

If you find the enemy encamped near the banks of a river
or lake, which you imagine they will attempt to cross for
their security upon being attacked, leave a detachment of
your party on the opposite shore to receive them, while,
with the remainder, you surprize them, having them
between you and the lake or river.

(Rogers, *Journals*, 63)

Water travel was such an essential element of the Rangers'
missions that Rogers concentrated his last five Ranging
Rules on tactics to be employed during operations carried out on
or near water. As we have discussed before, the Rangers had to
cross or navigate rivers, streams, and lakes during their many
scouting forays against the French. They were almost certain to
encounter parties of the enemy using these waterways as well. At
times, the sheer volume of traffic on the lakes prevented the
Rangers from continuing on their way, forcing them to wait for the
cover of night to hide their movements.

During a scout toward Crown Point in early May of 1756,
Rogers and his men, who were on foot, lay in ambush the whole
day and watched the amount of travel up the lake by the enemy:

We continued our march till the 5th of May, when I arrived with nine men at Lake Champlain, four miles south of Crown Point. Here we concealed our packs, and marched up to a village on the east-side, about two miles distant from Crown Point, but found no inhabitants there. We lay in wait the whole day following, opposite to Crown Point, expecting some party to cross the lake; but nothing appeared except about four or five hundred men in canoes and battoes, coming up the lake from St. Johns to Crown Point. (Rogers, *Journals*, 15)

Rogers knew from his experiences on the rivers and lakes that the enemy had encampments at different places along the shorelines and small islands. Rogers trained his men to try to catch the enemy "between two fires." By thinking ahead, calculating what the enemy's reaction to an attack would be, and placing his Rangers accordingly, he could take advantage of this foresight.

If the Rangers discovered a shoreline enemy encampment, Rogers advised them to post a detachment of some of their party on the opposite shore. If the enemy, when attacked, tried to escape to the other shore, the party waiting there could spring their ambush from the land while the rest of the Rangers chased after them in their boats, thereby catching the enemy "between two fires." The only path of retreat left to the enemy would be to try to outrun the Rangers in their boats. With the Rangers' skill in handling their boats and canoes, this method of escape would be very unlikely.

On their return from a scout to Ticonderoga, the Rangers were taking a view of the enemy's advanced guard at the north end of Lake George. They saw an enemy party stop on an island a few miles from them, but before they could form a plan of attack, the enemy embarked, heading straight toward the Ranger party:

While we were viewing these, I perceived a bark-canoe, with nine Indians and a Frenchman in it, going up the lake. We kept sight of them 'till they passed the point of land, where our canoe and men were left, where, when we arrived, we had information from our people, that the above Indians and Frenchman had landed on an island six miles to the south of us, near the middle of the lake. In a short time after, we saw them put off from the island, and steer directly towards us; upon which we put ourselves in readiness to receive them in the best manner we could, and gave them a salute at about 100 yards distance, which reduced their number to four. We then took boat and pursued them down the lake, till they were relieved by two canoes, which obliged us to retreat towards our encampment at Lake George, where we arrived the 10th of October. (Rogers, *Journals*, 3, 4)

With a little more time, the Rangers could have sprung a trap just as Rogers advised in Rule Number Twenty-Seven. This tactic did work on a scout in which Rogers left a party of his men on the shore under the command of Captain Putnam. Rogers and the rest of his force embarked in two boats and attacked an enemy party of thirty men in two canoes. In the ensuing battle on the water, the Rangers drove the enemy to within range of the party on shore, who gave them a brisk fire:

We steered as if we intended to pass by them, which luckily answered our expectations; for they boldly headed us till within about an hundred yards, when we discharged the before mentioned pieces, which killed several of them, and put the rest to flight, in which we drove them so near where our land-party lay, that they were again galled by them; several of the enemy tumbled into the water, and their canoes rendered very leaky. (Rogers, *Journals*, 6, 7)

The ability of the Rangers and the rest of the British Army to wage war upon the rivers and lakes was critical, as control of these bodies of water affected the ability of the army to move up Lakes George and Champlain toward the French forts at Ticonderoga and Crown Point. Later in the war, these waterways, along with the St. Lawrence River and Lake Ontario, would play a part in the British thrust to capture all of Canada. The French knew that they had to prevent the British Army from being able to come and go on these waterways as they pleased.

During the campaigns of 1757, the French were successful in stopping a force of New Jersey and New York Provincials on a scout upon Lake George:

On July 26, the French scored a critical victory near a spot on the lake called Sabbath Day Point. The New Jersey Regiment, or the Jersey Blues as they were more commonly known, was one of the best trained and equipped of the Provincial regiments. A combined force of Jersey Blues and New York Provincials were scouting down the lake near Sabbath Day Point when they were ambushed by a party of some 700 French and Indians led by Ensign Charles-Michel Mouet de Langlade. The Provincials were then pursued by Indians in canoes, and about 250 of Colonel John Parker's force of 350-400 men were killed, captured, or drowned. In addition, twenty-two valuable boats were lost. (Todish, 38)

This event illustrates the importance of control of the lakes and rivers, and the value of the watercraft that were used to travel upon them. Rogers understood this importance, and his rules reflect the need for tactics suited for use on the water or the land adjacent to it.

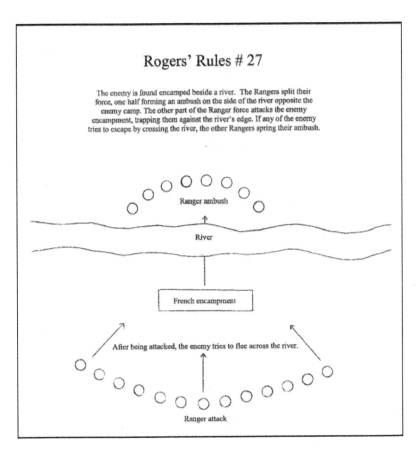

Rogers' Rules # 27

The enemy is found encamped beside a river. The Rangers split their
force, one half forming an ambush on the side of the river opposite the
enemy camp. The other part of the Ranger force attacks the enemy
encampment, trapping them against the river's edge. If any of the enemy
tries to escape by crossing the river, the other Rangers spring their ambush.

Ranger ambush

River

French encampment

After being attacked, the enemy tries to flee across the river.

Ranger attack

Figure 52. Ambush on the opposite shore.

Rogers' Rules: Number Twenty-Eight

If you cannot satisfy yourself as to the enemy's number and strength, from their fire, &c. conceal your boats at some distance, and ascertain their number by a reconnoitering party, when they embark, or march, in the morning, marking the course they steer, &c. when you may pursue, ambush, and attack them, or let them pass, as prudence shall direct you. In general, however, that you may not be discovered by the enemy on the lakes and rivers at a great distance, it is safest to lay by, with your boats and party concealed all day, without noise or shew, and to pursue your intended route by night; and whether you go by land or water, give out parole and countersigns, in order to know one another in the dark, and likewise appoint a station for every man to repair to, in case of any accident that may separate you.

(Rogers, *Journals*, 63, 64)

If the presence of the enemy was discovered from their fires, but their numbers could not be judged from this, Rogers advised his men to send a small scouting party to spy on the enemy when they continued their march in the morning. They were to gather as much information as possible in order to decide whether to attack or let the enemy pass because of superior numbers. By determining the course of the enemy's march, the Rangers might be able to get ahead of them and set an ambush at a spot better suited for it. Rogers repeatedly instructed his men to take advantage of the most appropriate ground for an ambush.

Rogers and his Rangers used every shred of information to gain a tactical advantage over the enemy:

> Sept. 7, 1756. Agreeable to orders, I this day embarked on Lake George, with a party of fourteen men in a whale-boat, which we landed, and concealed the evening following, on the east shore, about four miles south of the French advance guard. Here I divided my party, taking seven men with me leaving the remainder in charge of Mr. Chalmer (a volunteer sent me by Sir John Sinclair) with orders, upon his discovering the enemy's boats going up the lake &c. to make the best of his way with the intelligence to Fort William-Henry. (Rogers, *Journals*, 28, 29)

Another recurring theme in this rule is the tactic of traveling at night to prevent discovery by the enemy. The region around Lakes George and Champlain is very hilly and mountainous, providing many high vantage points from which to watch the travel of boats up and down the lakes. The Rangers took advantage of these elevated grounds on many occasions. If the Rangers traveled on the lakes during the day, the enemy would be able to see them and determine their numbers and course. This information would allow the enemy to form a judgment as to the Rangers' intended target, and possibly to set an ambush for them. By traveling at night, the Rangers were less likely to be seen, especially on the lakes:

> The following evening we embarked again, and went down the bay to within six miles of the French fort, where we concealed our boats till the evening. (Rogers, *Journals*, 18)

As the Rangers lay concealed during the day, they kept watch by posting the proper sentries and keeping an eye out for the advance of the enemy towards their hiding place. But they also gained vital details as to the movements of the enemy as they passed by. Time after time, we have seen how the information gathered by watching the movements and numbers of the enemy proved indispensable to the Rangers in carrying out their scouts. The time of day, the direction of travel, and the amount of provisions the enemy appeared to be carrying, all helped the Rangers decide how to proceed with their mission.

We can be assured that Rogers and his Rangers would have used many of his Ranging Rules to insure their safety as they lay in wait while the enemy moved by them, often so close that they could hear them talking, or watch them as they dined:

> At night we put off again, with a design to pass by Crown Point, but afterwards judged it imprudent by reason of the clearness of the night, to lay concealed again the next day, when near a hundred boats passed by us, seven of which came very near the point where we were, and would have landed there; but the officer insisted, in our hearing, upon going about 150 yards further, where they landed, and dined in our view. (Rogers, *Journals*, 19)

You can imagine the trepidation the Rangers must have felt the enemy approached their spot of concealment. This entry also points out another aspect of traveling by water at night. Most of the time, darkness would conceal the Rangers' movements, but in clear weather the moonlight could provide enough light to allow the enemy to see them upon the lakes. Thus, the Rangers even considered the weather and the moonlight when planning their missions.

Rogers' *Journals* contain many accounts in which the Rangers used boats to travel quickly along the rivers or lakes, but then, when they got close to the enemy, factors dictated that they would have to make the rest of their trip by marching overland. Three New Hampshire soldiers recorded this information from a scout toward Fort St. Frederick:

> Set forward in a Battoe from the Encampment, the 14th Sept. at about 25 miles distance down the Lake, landed about daylight, took Battoe out & hid it, left two men of Connecticut Forces there to watch the Battoe, & Provisions till our return, Saw, that morning, Sundry Indian Canoes

passing in the lower part of the Lake. Went forward towards Crown Point. (Hall, 35)

No doubt the amount of traffic by the Indians in their canoes caused Rogers to hide his boat and continue his march by land towards Crown Point.

Whether traveling by water or land, or by day or night, Rogers trained the Rangers to be prepared for any action with the enemy, or accident that might cause the Rangers to be separated from each other. We have already discussed Rogers' tactic of appointing several places to rendezvous in case of being broken in an action with the enemy, or if some other circumstances separated the Rangers. By doing this, the men could regroup at this appointed place and make new dispositions of the men in case the enemy was pursuing them. The Rangers could decide at this point to continue their mission or to return to their base if the circumstances so dictated. The loss of even a single man to the enemy could spell disaster for the scout. Information gained from this prisoner could lead to an ambush of the Ranger party, or even the loss of the entire force. To combat this, Rogers also instructed his Rangers to appoint countersigns and paroles so they could identify each other, especially in the event of a separation or when traveling at night when it would be harder to distinguish friend from foe.

We have already discussed how on one occasion some of the Rangers, when returning from a scout, were challenged by the encampment's sentries. But circumstances led to the Rangers not hearing the challenge, so the sentry, who feared that the approaching Rangers were the enemy, shot them. By establishing countersigns, the Rangers could be certain that the men approaching were indeed friendly, thus avoiding the confusion that might lead to accidental shootings:

Wednesday, 2d. – This morning Major Putnam's men had ten days rations dealt out to them and Major Rogers had as much for his men. And there was about 100 of the regulars and about 150 of the light infantry and about 400 of the rangers and they got their men served with provisions and landed them on the shore and marched off about 9 o'clock. And they was drawed up in three columns when they marched and Major Rogers marched in the front and Major Putnam on the rear. And the counter sign for the scout was Boston. That was, if any man should hail you, you must answer Boston, and if you hailed anybody and they did not answer Boston, you must take them to be an enemy. And we marched till we came to a place where Rogers encamped with a scout about a month before, which was about half way from the lake to South Bay. (Todish /Zaboly, 133)

We can see by this entry how something as simple as a countersign or parole could save the life of a fellow soldier. With the possibility of becoming engaged with the enemy so great when operating in their territory, the foresight of establishing tactics to prevent accidents between fellow soldiers is another example of trying to think ahead and be prepared for any eventuality that may occur.

Epilogue

Such in general are the rules to be observed in the Ranging service; there are, however, a thousand occurrences and circumstances which may happen, that will make it necessary, in some measure to depart from them, and put other arts and stratagems in practice; and which cases every man's reason and judgment must be his guide, according to the particular situation and nature of things; and that he may do this to advantage, he should keep in mind a maxim never to be departed from by a commander, viz. to preserve a firmness and presence of mind on every occasion.

(Rogers, *Journals*, 64)

As thorough as he tried to be, Robert Rogers realized that there would be circumstances that would require the Rangers to deviate from his Rules by using different tactics that seemed better suited to the individual situation. Indeed, part of the Rangers' training entailed making quick decisions to counter the enemy's movements or attacks. This training would allow the Rangers to deal with situations that were out of the ordinary. This is the reason that Rogers advised his men to rely on their own reasoning and best judgment when dealing with the enemy on their scouts.

An example of underlying factors that caused a deviation from one of Rogers' Rules was when Rogers decided to march back by the same path into an ambush that led to the "First Battle on Snowshoes." The fact that the Rangers' guns were soaking wet played a big part in Rogers' decision to break one of his own rules. Had the Rangers not returned to the place of their previous night's fires to dry their muskets, the history of the Ranging service may have ended then and there, with the possible death of its leader.

The condition of the men, the amount of provisions and ammunition that they had left, and the distance they were from their home base could all play a large part in their decision making. Rogers' Rules were just part of a bold revolution that was starting to develop in the late seventeenth and early eighteenth centuries. The usefulness of lightly burdened, quick moving parties of men who could sustain themselves in all kinds of terrain without dependence on supply from the main army, was a concept that was growing in popularity, and Rogers, with his set of Ranging Rules, did much to further this idea.

Many of the early Rangers were frontier bred, a fact that had great bearing on the early successes of their scouting and intelligence gathering missions. Being able to sustain themselves in the woods by relying on the skills they learned as hunters and trappers would prove to be an essential part of their very existence. The ability to travel over all kinds of terrain, in all kinds of weather, using whatever equipment would give them an advantage over the enemy, would become a hallmark of the Ranger Companies.

Another thing that Rogers stressed in his conclusion was that a steady mind was necessary by the officers present on a scout or action for any chance of its success. An officer who panicked would soon lead to a general disintegration of the force he commanded. Clear, concise orders, given with certain firmness, would instill confidence in the men and increase their willingness to carry out those orders. If the men did not trust their officers, they would be reluctant to follow them into the enemy's territory.

In many of Rogers' orders, he stressed the need for the party to be headed by "proper officers, of whom you can confide." In the eighteenth century, the ability of the officers to guide their men on the battlefield was critical. Historical references are full of instances where the loss of an officer, or the inability of an officer to lead, spelled disaster for the troops under their command. The death of Lord Howe during the 1758 Campaign against Ticonderoga, and Abercromby's subsequent retreat, is perhaps the best example of how the lack of a steady, well-respected officer could mean the difference between victory and defeat.

Another way Rogers tried to gain an advantage for his men was in the clothing that they wore. Although the term "camouflage," as we know it today, was not used, the practice of wearing clothing that blended into the surroundings had been used for many years. In Captain John Knox's descriptions of the early Ranger companies, the Rangers had no issued uniforms, but wore their clothes short. The shorter clothing made it easier to travel through the woods. When the Rangers were issued uniforms in early 1758, Rogers ordered them to be made of "green Bath rug, and cheap green cloths." The use of green and other dark or earth tone colors gave the Rangers another tactical advantage in the woods. Elements of the Indian style of dress, such as "leggings" became a vital part of the Rangers' clothing. While the Rangers never had an established uniform that was used by all the companies during the course of the war, the clothes they wore began to influence the uniforms of the British Regular troops. The length of the Regulars' uniforms grew shorter and shorter, and Gage's Light Infantrymen wore uniforms of brown, a real departure from the "madder red" of the British Army.

Even the personal appearance of the Rangers could be used to a tactical advantage when in the woods, trying to move undiscovered by the enemy:

> Although most British soldiers of the period were clean shaven, Light Infantrymen were encouraged to develop a "smutted" appearance for better concealment in the woods. (McCulloch/Todish, *British Light Infantryman*, 62)

Eighteenth-century men did not normally wear beards and mustaches, but when spending many days out on the trail trying to elude the enemy, the Rangers often accumulated several days' growth of beard between shavings. A historical reference to the appearance of some Light Infantrymen during the 1758 Louisbourg campaign describes the sometimes-periodic shaving habits of His Majesty's troops:

> The beard of their upper Lips, some grown into whiskers, others not so, but all well smutted on that part. (McCulloch/Todish, *British Light Infantryman*, 15)

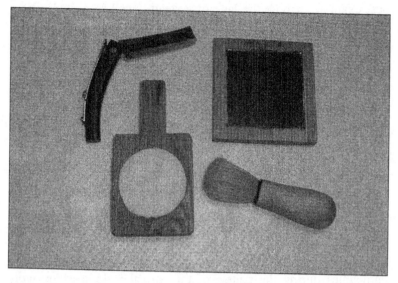

Figure 53. A reproduction shaving kit of the style used by eighteenth-century soldiers. A hand carved shaving soap block, shaving brush, folding razor, and a small mirror round out the kit.

While the above account refers to the appearance of the Light Infantry, we know that they tried to emulate the Rangers by altering their uniforms and gear, and by adopting many of the Rangers' tactics.

The student of Rogers' Rules soon discovers an underlying theme: be prepared. Rogers instructed his men to be prepared and alert at all times, so that the enemy would have a hard time in catching them by surprise. If they *were* caught by surprise, the Rangers' quick reactions could turn a possible defeat into a stalemate, or even a victory.

Whether in their encampments, marching formations, or boats upon the water, the Rangers used every advantage possible to secure them from an enemy attack. Their ability to march at a moment's notice, carry more ammunition than a Regular soldier, and use it expertly, was another trait of these daring raiders. They could travel in all sorts of weather and over many different types of ground, which allowed the Rangers to carry on the British war effort, even in winter, while the Regulars were safe in their beds.

The French raiders knew that the Rangers could be on their trails like bloodhounds at a moment's notice. While sometimes deserving of the term "savage" in their appearance, method of fighting, and dress, the Rangers were also called some of best soldiers to take up the British cause.

As we have discussed before, while Rogers did not invent the concept of the "Rangers," he and his Ranging Rules probably did more to further the development of "Light Troops" and "Special Forces" than we will ever know. The conversion to the tactics of woodland warfare forever changed the makeup of the armed forces. Units of "Light Troops" evolved during subsequent conflicts and wars, leading to the establishment of the United States Army Rangers and other elite units like the Navy Seals. These units are to this day, a vital and permanent part of the United States Armed Forces. The skills and techniques developed by these "Special Forces" can be directly attributed to Robert Rogers and his Ranging Companies of the French and Indian War. The use of special equipment and weapons, unique tactical training, and the ability to strike quickly while maintaining a heavy and constant fire against the enemy, echoes the words Robert Rogers drummed into the heads of his Rangers. Robert Rogers, and his Rules for the Ranging Service, are a timeless legacy.

Figure 54. The author is dressed in the green uniform coat such as Robert Rogers ordered for some of his companies after Lord Loudon augmented the Ranger Corps in the 1758 establishment. Rogers favored "green Bath Rugg, and cheap green cloths" for the wool uniform coats, according to references from the sutlers contracted for the clothing. This color allowed the Rangers to hide from, and avoid detection in the woods by their enemies more easily than Regular soldiers wearing the red uniforms of the British Army.

Appendix

Eighteenth-Century Flintlock Muskets

During the course of the French and Indian War, the Rangers used a variety of flintlock muskets and rifles. These weapons were available to them either from the British Army or from the merchants, or "sutlers," that were attached to the army. The "establishments," or enlistment terms, for the years 1756, 1757, and 1758 all required the enlisting men to find their own arms:

> Your men to find their own arms, which must be such as upon examination, shall be found fit, and be approved of. (Todish/Zaboly, 87)

The standard military musket of the day was known as the "King's Arm." Today it is commonly called by its nickname, the "Brown Bess." (This term may not have originated until the Revolutionary War period.) This musket featured a 46-inch long smoothbore barrel of .75 caliber, brass or iron mounting, flintlock ignition, and a full-length walnut stock. Eighteenth-century rifles were considered more accurate than smoothbore muskets, because the inside of a rifle's barrel was grooved with spirals that imparted spin to the lead ball. The disadvantage of a rifle was that it took considerably more time to reload than a smoothbore musket. Eighteenth-century military tactics, however, did not rely on accuracy but rather on speed in reloading, to which muskets were better suited. By delivering volleys of musket fire, the rigid columns of infantrymen attempted to literally drive their opponents off the field of battle. During the latter parts of the war, the British Army started to understand the advantages of equipping a certain number of skilled marksmen with rifled-barreled guns to combat their enemy:

> Light Infantrymen with good shooting skills prior to the Ticonderoga expedition of 1758 found themselves issued with a new weapon before the campaign. Eighty "riffled barrel pieces" of European origin were given to the ten best shots in Major General James Abercromby's large army. (McCulloch/Todish, *British Light Infantryman*, 19)

If the Rangers were not issued a standard military musket, they would have had to find or buy their own arms. Many of the Rangers brought their own personal hunting weapons with them when they enlisted. If a Ranger's own firearm was approved for use, he was sometimes even paid a bounty for it. If the enlisting Rangers did not bring their personal weapons with them, there was a great variety of arms available to them from the local merchants and army sutlers:

> For instance, John Pim's on Anne Street sold, "at very Reasonable Rates, Sundry sorts of choice Arms lately arrived from London, viz., Handy Muskets, Buccaneer-Guns, Fowling pieces, Hunting Guns, Carabines, Several sorts of Pistols, Brass and Iron," and so on. (Zaboly, *A True Ranger*, 14)

A smoothbore hunting weapon, or "fusil," would have been many Rangers' weapon of choice. The smoothbore fusil could be reloaded more quickly than a rifle, and many would deliver better accuracy than the standard military muskets. A very loose-fitting lead ball, quite a bit smaller than the musket's bore, was used in the military muskets to aid in reloading after the musket became fouled. The blackpowder propellant of the day left a large amount of residue behind in the barrel after firing; as much as fifty percent of the powder charge.

The British Army employed armorers, or men whose duty it was to repair damaged weapons and equipment, but small repairs and general maintenance of a Ranger's firelock would have been his own responsibility, especially when out in the field. The Rangers, especially the company sergeants, would have carried a few special tools, as well as items to clean and maintain their arms. Spare springs, and small, easily lost screws may have been carried as well.

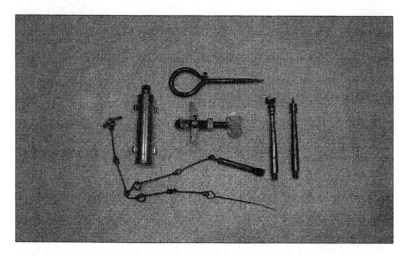

Figure 55. Some of the tools the Rangers might have carried to service and maintain their firelocks. A turn screw, a tin oil bottle, a spring vise, a worm for cleaning the barrel, a ball screw for removing a charge without firing the musket, and a whisk and pick for cleaning the pan of the flintlock.

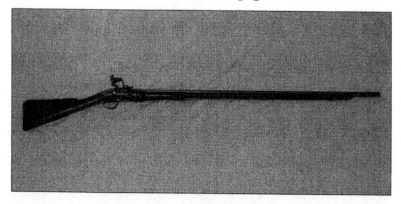

Figure 56. An original musket manufactured from 1715 to 1720. This musket was built by a private gun maker for the British Army.

Prior to the British Army's 1728 Warrant that established a standardized musket, the colonels of the different British regiments were required to contract on their own for their men's arms. This meant that there could be many differences from regiment to regiment in the way the muskets were built. After the 1728 Warrant, every musket was to be built using standardized parts that were manufactured to the same specifications and built to the same standards, so that all of the regiments in the British Army would be armed with the same muskets.

This musket features an English walnut stock, a 46-inch long, .77 caliber smoothbore barrel, iron mountings, a banana shaped lock assembly, and a wooden ramrod. As the newer, standardized muskets began to be issued to the British regiments, the older muskets, such as this one, were issued to Provincial regiments, and some even found their way into some of the Provincial Ranger companies. This musket belongs to the Ohio Historical Society, and is housed in the collection at the Fort Laurens Historical site, located in Zoar, Ohio. Fort Laurens, the only fort built in the Ohio Territory during the Revolutionary War, had been established as a supply post to support the 1778 campaign against the British at Fort Detroit in the Michigan Territory. The poorly supplied colonials would have been issued "hand-me-down" muskets like these if they were enrolled in the local militia units. Muskets like this one, predating the French and Indian War, still would have been in use during the fight for American independence.

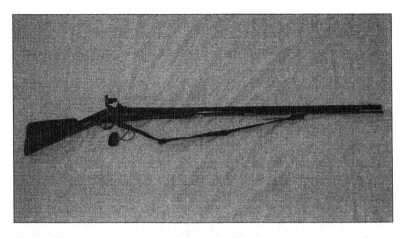

Figure 57. A reproduction First Model King's Arm, or "Brown Bess" musket that was the standard issue military firelock of the French and Indian War. It features an English walnut stock, .75 caliber 46-inch long smoothbore barrel, brass mountings, banana shaped flintlock assembly, sling swivels, and sling, and a wooden ramrod. The overall length of this musket was 62 ½ inches long, and it weighed 9 pounds. These muskets were manufactured from 1730 to the 1740s.

The Brown Bess, with its standardized parts and the newly developed socket bayonet, which allowed the soldier to fire and reload his musket while the bayonet was attached, or "fixed," greatly revolutionized the military tactics used by Regular troops during the eighteenth century. The barrel of this musket was "browned," or darkened so the light would not reflect off its once shiny barrel and reveal its user. British Regular troops were required to keep the barrels and other hardware on their muskets "bright," or shiny. Regulars carried brick dust with them in their kits to use as a polishing. The Rangers were known for darkening their barrels, and the evolving Light Infantry companies were ordered to "blacken," their barrels to prevent the sun glinting off them, and to improve the sight picture along the barrel.

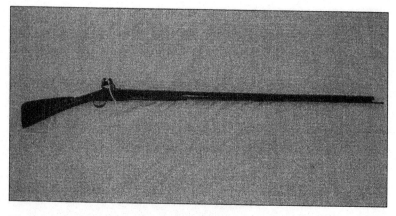

Figure 58.   A reproduction French "fusil fin." This was a finely made hunting weapon, used by many colonials to protect and provide for their families. The lock, sideplate, and trigger guard are beautifully engraved. This musket features a very long 48-inch long, .62 caliber smoothbore barrel, iron mountings, and wooden ramrod.   This would have been a personal firearm, now used for war. The length of the barrel, huge by today's standards, was very common in the colonial period. Many period muskets were of this style.

The barrel of a musket was required to be at least three and a half feet long, in order to be approved for use in Colonial militia units. Muskets of this type were known as "trade guns," because they were primarily built as a trade item for the Native Americans. Many of the natives preferred the more elaborately engraved and decorated locks, sideplates, and trigger guards, specifying them when trading for a musket. Some sideplates were even made in the form of serpents, another item especially desired by the natives. These trade guns were a vital part of the fur trade that was one of the most important commercial ventures in the colonies and on the frontiers. A trade gun like this reproduction would have been available from many of the traders servicing the colonies, or even could have been a captured weapon, such as the French muskets that Captain John Lovewell and his party of New England Rangers captured while on a scalp hunting mission, February 20th, 1725. The party of Rangers later sold the French muskets for 70 pounds. These muskets then would have been available for sale by the buyers in Massachusetts.

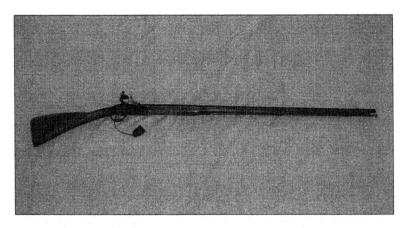

Figure 59. A reproduction Tulle "fusil de chasse," or "gun of the hunt." The original models were manufactured at the arsenal in Tulle, France. This was the common workingman's gun, which was used to feed and protect his family. This is another of the common "trade guns" available for the fur trade, specifically targeting trade with the Native Americans. This gun features a cherry wood stock, a 42-inch long .62 caliber smoothbore barrel, iron mountings, wooden ramrod, and flintlock ignition. Part of the versatility of a weapon like this, with its smoothbore barrel, is its ability to shoot both a round lead ball, and buckshot. This allowed it to be used for both large and small game, as well as the many birds, and waterfowl hunted in the eighteenth century. This would have also allowed the Rangers to shoot their normal "buck and ball" load. Many of the Rangers would have brought weapons like these with them when enlisting, and would have received "bounty money," for them if they were approved for use.

One problem that arose from the use of personal weapons, was that the standard British military ammunition did not fit these muskets. The men had to "cast" their own lead ball from personal bullet molds. The discovery of lead casting sprue on Rogers Island lends credence to the theory that many of the Rangers used weapons like this.

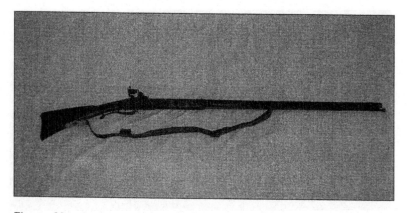

Figure 60.   A reproduction American colonial fowler, another personal hunting weapon that an enlisting soldier may have brought with him from home, now to be used in the war.

This fowler, which is a .75 caliber smoothbore, features an American striped maple stock, and hardware, and mountings, such as the triggerguard, and sideplate, that show some of the Germanic influence in the American colonies at the time, which would eventually develop into what we know as the "American Longrifle." This musket has had some modifications done to it, to make it more suitable for military use, by the addition of a sling, and a British issue "hammer cap," a piece of leather to cover the frizzen of the flintlock to prevent an accidental discharge of the musket when priming and loading with a paper cartridge. This musket, built with a .75 caliber smoothbore barrel, would have been able to use standard British military ammunition. Again, the smoothbore barrel would have allowed the use of a lead ball for large game, or buckshot for small game and waterfowl.

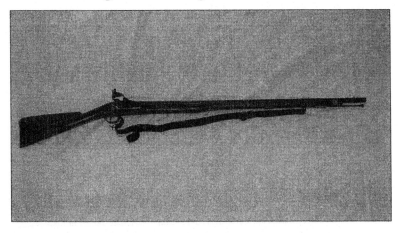

Figure 61. A reproduction "officer's fusil," or what was a scaled down version of the British Army's standard firelock, the First Model King's Arm. This musket features a 39-inch long, .66 caliber smoothbore barrel, an English walnut stock, brass mountings, a bayonet lug, sling swivels and sling, and an iron ramrod.

In early 1759, Rogers received an order of arms from Mr. Cunningham, a sutler to the Rangers. While no description of these arms is known to exist today, many historians believe they might have been smaller caliber, smoothbore "carbines," such as the reproduction shown above. It is known that some smooth-bored "Light Infantry Carbines" were introduced in 1757. A historical reference to the Rangers by a captain in the 27th Regiment states that the Rangers were armed mostly with rifles. As we have discussed in a previous chapter, 300 rifle-barreled carbines with bayonets and iron ramrods were ordered for the 60th Royal American Regiment in early 1757. As the British Army began to develop new tactics, ten rifle-barrel carbines were issued to the ten best marksmen in each company. While an example of this type of original firelock is not known to exist at this time, many historians believe that they would have been of the style and build of the reproduction pictured here.

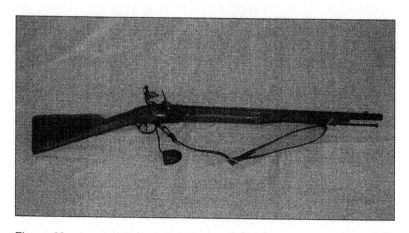

Figure 62. A reproduction of a severely shortened Brown Bess musket. This musket originally sported a 42-inch long barrel, but has been shortened to make it easier to use in the woodlands in which the Rangers operated. The Rangers were known to shorten their muskets, and to even dress down the wooden stocks to make them lighter.

Cut-off barrel sections ranging from four to eight inches long have been unearthed on Rogers Island, and are attributed to the Rangers shortening their barrels. The accompanying photograph shows the second model of the standard British military musket, or "Brown Bess," which was developed in 1768, so it would not have been available to the Rangers during the French and Indian War. It probably saw limited use in the colonies even during the Revolutionary War. It had a shorter, 42-inch long, .75 caliber barrel, with a walnut stock and an iron ramrod. It is shown here because its barrel has been shortened a full twelve inches, back to an overall barrel length of 30 inches. The Native Americans were known for shortening their muskets like this, even going as far as cutting off the end of the wooden stocks to better enable them to hide them under their blankets, and to use them from canoes.

A Note to Reenactors

Each year thousands of reenactors attend historical reenactments, present historical programs for schoolchildren, and otherwise share their love for history with the public. For the last seven years, I have been a member of the Ohio Company of Jaeger's Battalion, the world's largest and oldest recreated unit of Rogers' Rangers of the French and Indian War. Information gathered over these seven years, by attending events at some of the historic sites dedicated to the preservation of the French and Indian War period, became a vital part of this book.

Some of these sites include, Fort No. 4, Charlestown, New Hampshire; Johnson Hall, Johnstown, New York; Fort Johnson, Fort Johnson, New York; The Crown Point Historic Site, Crown Point, New York; Fort Klock, St. Johnsville, New York; Mount Defiance, Ticonderoga, New York; Fort Michilimackinac, Mackinaw City, Michigan; Old Fort Niagara, Youngstown, New York; Rogers Island, Fort Edward, New York; Rogers Rock, Hague, New York; Fort Stanwix, Rome, New York; Fort Ticonderoga, Ticonderoga, New York; and Fort William Henry in the Village of Lake George, New York. I would be remiss not to mention Lakes Champlain and George, as well as the Mohawk River Valley and the Adirondack Mountains, some of the most beautiful country I have ever had the pleasure of traveling through. Each of these historic sites preserves the windows to our past. We should be thankful to the people involved in the past, present, and future support of these landmarks in our nation's history.

Most of these sites have displays and collections, some large and some small, in their visitor centers or museum facilities. These displays and collections give us a unique perspective on some of the items used in the daily lives of our forefathers. To the modern day reenactor, these collections are another way for us to investigate, research, and better portray the persons we are trying to bring back to life. Preserving these artifacts is a costly, time-consuming job, but one that is essential to help us in our understanding of times past.

Another way that we reenactors can better understand and represent our chosen time periods, is through the reproduction uniforms, weapons, and gear we use during our reenactments. Each piece must be carefully researched and documented when possible, in order to provide the most accurate information to the public, many of whom are schoolchildren. Without the interest of the young people, our past will be forgotten. Wearing wool uniforms in unbearable heat or cold, while carrying and using the accoutrements of an eighteenth-century soldier, allows us another way of looking at the trials of those who came before us. By actually getting out and using these pieces of gear, we can learn what would have, and would not have worked. The failure of an important piece of gear could leave a man sick, frostbitten, or even dead.

Attending historical events enriches your reenacting experience by spending time with other people who share your passion for recreating history. The information that can be gleaned from the countless debates, sometimes heated, would fill volumes. A reenactor will be the first to tell you if something can be documented or not. You never know when someone will uncover that hidden piece to a historical puzzle that you have been trying to solve.

The diagrams in this book are movements assumed to have been used by Rogers and his Rangers, based on historical references. The diagrams attempt to show on paper what Rogers felt would have worked best when confronted by the enemy, or in other situations that developed during some of the Rangers' scouting missions.

As Rogers himself cautioned, his Ranging Rules would not cover all circumstances, but would be a good start when combined with a cool, steady head and a healthy dose of common sense. This may be the greatest lesson we modern reenactors can learn from Major Rogers.

Bibliography

Anderson, Fred. *Crucible of War: The Seven Years' War and the Fate of Empire in British North America 1754-1766*. New York: Alfred A. Knopf, 2000.

Bellico, Russell P. *Sails and Steam in the Mountains: A Maritime and Military History of Lake George and Lake Champlain*. Fleischmanns, NY: Purple Mountain Press, Revised edition, 2001.

Bland, Humphrey. *A Treatise of Military Discipline in which is Laid Down and Explained the Duty of the Soldier, through the Several Branches of the Service*. London: printed for R. Baldwin, J. Richardson, T. Longman, H. Woodgate, and S. Brooks, 1759.

Cuneo, John R. *Robert Rogers of the Rangers*. Ticonderoga, NY: Fort Ticonderoga Museum, 1988.

Hall, Dennis Jay. *The Journals of Sir William Johnson's Scouts, 1755 & 1756*. Panton, VT: Essence of Vermont, 1999.

Henry, Alexander, edited by David A. Armour. *Attack at Michilimackinac: Alexander Henry's Travels and Adventures in Canada and the Indian Territories Between the Years 1760 and 1764*. New York: I. Riley, 1971.

Kayworth Alfred E. and Raymond G. Potvin. *The Scalp Hunters: Abenaki Ambush at Lovewell Pond, 1725*. Wellesley, MA: Branden Books, a Division of Branden Publishing Company, 2002.

Kemmer, Brenton C. *Redcoats, Yankees, and Allies: A History of the Uniforms, Clothing, and Gear of the British Army in the Lake George-Lake Champlain Corridor, 1755-1760.* Bowie, MD: Heritage Books, Inc., 1998.

Knox, John, edited by Arthur G. Doughty. *An Historical Journal of the Campaigns in North America for the Years 1757, 1758, 1759, and 1760.* Published in three volumes. Toronto, Canada: The Champlain Society, 1914.

Knox, Captain John, edited and introduced by Brian Connell. *The Siege of Quebec and Other Campaigns in North America, 1757-1760.* London: The Folio Society, 1976.

Loescher, Burt Garfield. *The History of Rogers' Rangers: Volume I, The Beginnings.* Facsimile Reprint. Bowie, MD: Heritage Books, Inc., 2001

Loescher, Burt Garfield. *The History of Rogers' Rangers: Volume II, Genesis: Rogers' Rangers–The First Green Berets. The Corps and the Revivals: April 6, 1758-December 24, 1783.* Facsimile reprint with additional illustrations. Bowie, MD: Heritage Books, Inc., 2000.

Loescher, Burt Garfield. *The History of Rogers' Rangers: Volume 4, The St. Francis Raid.* Bowie, MD: Heritage Books, Inc., 2002.

Marrin, Albert. *Struggle for a Continent: The French and Indian Wars, 1690-1760.* New York: Macmillan Publishing Company, Collier Macmillan Canada, Inc., 1987.

McCulloch, Ian M. and Todish, Timothy J. *British Light Infantryman of the Seven Years War. North America 1757-63* Osprey Publishing Warrior Series 88. London: Osprey Publishing Ltd., 2004.

McCulloch, Ian and Todish, Timothy J. *Through So Many Dangers: The Memoirs and Adventures of Robert Kirk, Late of the Royal Highland Regiment.* Fleischmanns, NY: Purple Mountain Press, Ltd., 2004.

Matheney, Chris. "Perspective Glasses: Notes from the Ordnance Depot." *The Battalion Journal.* January 2002, issue #22.

Moody, Thomas, and P. M. Woodwell, editor. *The Diary of Thomas Moody: Campaign of 1760 of the French & Indian War.* South Berwick, ME: 1976.

Parkman, Francis. *Montcalm and Wolfe: The French and Indian War.* New York: De Capo Press, Inc., a Subsidiary of Plenum Publishing Corporation, 1995.

Peckham, Howard H. *The Colonial Wars, 1689-1762.* Chicago and London: The University of Chicago Press, 1964.

Pray, Thomas. "Box or Bag?" *The Battalion Journal.* April 2004, issue #31.

Rogers, Robert. *The Journals of Major Robert Rogers.* Reprint of the 1769 Dublin edition. Published as *Warfare on the Colonial American Frontier: The Journals of Major Robert Rogers & An Historical Account of the Expedition Against the Ohio Indians in the Year 1764, Under the Command of Henry Bouquet, Esq.* Bargersville, Indiana: Dresslar Publishing, 1997.

Rogers, Robert J. *Rising Above Circumstances: The Rogers Family in Colonial America.* Quebec, Canada: Sheltus & Picard Inc., 1998.

Starbuck, David R. *The Great Warpath: British Military Sites from Albany to Crown Point.* Hanover, NH: University Press of New England, 1999.

Stott, Earl. *Exploring Rogers Island*. Fort Edward, NY: The Rogers Island Historical Association, 1969.

Todish, Timothy J. *America's* First *First World War: The French and Indian War, 1754-1763*. Flieschmanns, NY: Purple Mountain Press, Ltd., 2002.

Todish, Timothy J. and Gary S. Zaboly. *The Annotated and Illustrated Journals of Major Robert Rogers*. Flieschmanns, NY: Purple Mountain Press, Ltd., 2002.

Zaboly, Gary. *American Colonial Ranger. The Northern Colonies 1724-64*. The Warrior Series, 85. London: Osprey Publishing Ltd., 2004.

Zaboly, Gary. *A True Ranger: The Life and Many Wars of Major Robert Rogers*. Garden City Park, NY: Royal Blockhouse llc., 2004.

Index

About the Author

M att Wulff is an industrial mechanic, welder, and fabricator, having worked in this capacity for the Johns Manville Corporation for the last twenty-one years. A lifelong love of history, which started out with the Davy Crockett and Daniel Boone television eras, led Matt to become involved in historical reenacting, the last seven years as a member of Jaeger's Battalion, the world's oldest and largest recreated Rogers' Rangers unit in the country. Matt and Beth, his wife of twenty-four years, attend French and Indian War events all over the country, helping to educate the public about this important part of the development of what would become the United States. Truly a family affair, Matt and Beth are at times joined by their daughter, Brittany and son, Michael and daughter-in-law, Heather.

Research toward the goal of recreating a Ranger of the French and Indian War as historically correct as possible, and historical papers written while obtaining his "Senior Ranger Award," a specialized program within Jaeger's Battalion designed to test and improve a member's skills and understanding of Rogers' Rangers, led Matt to try his hand at writing historical articles for publication. Matt has had articles published in the *Battalion Journal* (the quarterly journal of Jaeger's Battalion), *Smoke and Fire News,* and *Muzzleloader* magazine. This is Matt's first book.

CPSIA information can be obtained at www.ICGtesting.com
Printed in the USA
BVOW06s0353010915

415182BV00008B/99/P